What They Ha...
Their Personality Traits,
Their Childhood Histories,
And Their Horrifying,
Murderous Techniques...

➤

Here are the killers, the crimes, and why they killed.

There was ALBERT DESALVO, "The Boston Strangler," who pinned the blame for 13 murders and rapes on his insatiable sexual desire. CHARLES RILEY who claimed his girlfriend had total power over him, and drove him to murder her parents. RONALD DEFEO who shot his family to death and said the devil made him do it. And RICHARD SPECK. Was brain damage the reason why he brutally murdered eight women?

FROM NEW YORK'S "SON OF SAM" TO L.A.'s "HILLSIDE STRANGLER," SHOCKING INSIGHT INTO THE MINDS OF AMERICA'S WORST KILLERS...

➤

WHY THEY KILLED

Jean F. Blashfield

POPULAR LIBRARY

An Imprint of Warner Books, Inc

A Time Warner Company

POPULAR LIBRARY EDITION

Copyright © 1990 by Jean Blashfield Black
All rights reserved.

Cover design by Amy King
Cover photos by Bettman Archives/Associated Press

Popular Library books are published by
Warner Books, Inc.
666 Fifth Avenue
New York, N.Y. 10103

A Time Warner Company

Printed in the United States of America

First Printing: November, 1990

10 9 8 7 6 5 4 3 2 1

This book is for my niece,
Christine Graf Loots,
who might well write the next one

And thanks to:
Jay Robert Nash, who provided considerable impetus to this project.

Christine Graf Loots, who helped with the Arizona research.

The librarians without whom this book wouldn't have happened, especially those at:
University of Oregon Library, Eugene, Oregon
Denver Public Library, Denver, Colorado
In Wisconsin:
  University of Wisconsin at Whitewater Library
  Janesville Public Library
  Waukesha Public Library
  Lake Geneva Public Library
  Barrett Library, Williams Bay
  Walworth Public Library

My agents, Scott and Barbara Siegel, who helped me after an ungainly fall on a Washington, D.C., street and became friends.

And to my husband, Wally Black, and children, Winston and Chandelle, for their patience and love during the long hours it took to write this book.

Contents

Introduction

"My wife's been shot. I've been shot," said the pained voice of the caller to the 911 Boston police dispatcher. It was late at night on October 23, 1989.

The voice faded before the dispatcher could find out where the man was calling from. The police had to follow the sound of their own sirens as it came over the victim's car phone into the dispatcher's ears. When they located the car, it was in a neighborhood populated predominately by blacks. Charles Stuart lay crumpled in the front seat, bleeding heavily from a bullet wound in his abdomen. Beside him lay his attractive lawyer wife, seven months pregnant, with a bullet in her head. Their son would be born by cesarean section performed on her dying body. The boy would live only seventeen days.

After long hours of surgery to repair the damage to his abdomen, a sobbing Stuart told the police that he and his wife, on leaving a childbirth class at a women's hospital, had been approached by a black man dressed in a jogging suit and holding a gun. Their assailant forced them to drive into the Mission Hill district, where he took their money and jewelry and then shot the two of them.

An intensive manhunt for a black killer, a hunt that violated numerous rights of citizens in the black community, brought out usually hidden racial fears felt by many white urban residents. What they were not to learn for more than two months was that Charles Stuart himself had apparently killed his wife in a carefully engineered plan.

The day after an unemployed thirty-nine-year-old black man was blamed for the murder, Stuart's brother, Matthew, went to the police. He told them that Charles had asked him to get rid of the gun used to murder his wife, as well as her purse containing the jewelry. Then his brother had apparently returned to the car and shot himself—wounding himself much more severely than he intended.

Hours after Matthew started talking, in the hours before dawn, Charles Stuart went to a 145-foot-high bridge over Boston Harbor and jumped to his death. He left a note which said in part, "The last four months have been real hell. . . . In our souls, we must forgive the sinner, because He would."

Now, with the alleged killer dead, the public began to ask why Stuart had not been investigated in the first place. Friends and family members came forward to say that Charles Stuart had been asking them for advice on how to kill his wife after she had refused to have an abortion. Apparently those friends didn't take him seriously.

We can probably never know the whole story of why Charles Stuart allegedly killed his wife and unborn son. However, apparently the "trigger"—the superficial "why" that police departments and newspapers usually accept as a motive—was that Carol was attracted by the possibility of not going back to work after the baby was born. Chuck had ambitions of owning his own top-quality restaurant, preferably as soon as possible, and loss of his attorney-wife's income would slow the realization of that ambition. By killing her, he expected to get a great deal of insurance money that would let him start up his own business sooner.

The "trigger" is the outer layer of why a murderer kills, the reason that is superficially obvious, the reason that is most often used in court by the prosecution. It can be as straightforward as the greed that Charles Stuart apparently felt. In the case of many street criminals who murder, the trigger is probably the knowledge that the person they have robbed could identify them, or rage at not finding any money, so that they kill the robbery victim. In the case of a love triangle, one spouse may kill the other out of jealousy or a desire to marry the other woman.

Beneath that trigger is the layer of hidden motivations. These are the "whys" that we will look at more closely in this book.

Martin Daly and Margo Wilson in the 1988 book *Homicide* enumerated a few such "whys" along with some societal influences: "Why do people kill one another? ... Because violent people were themselves abused in childhood. Because of envy engendered by social inequities. Because the penalties are not severe enough. Because of brain tumors, hormone imbalances, and alcohol-induced psychoses. Because modern weapons bypass our natural face-to-face inhibitions and empathies. Because of the violence on TV. ..." That list makes the "whys" seem endless and perpetually fascinating.

In the case of Charles Stuart, his hidden motivations probably stemmed from his blue-collar upbringing. He mentioned to one friend that he thought Carol was getting "the upper hand" in their marriage. Perhaps, rooted in his childhood, he had an overwhelming notion that any man who was a man would never allow his wife to dictate any of the important circumstances of their life and marriage. Or perhaps the man who at twenty was a short-order cook and at twenty-nine was the $100,000-a-year manager of a society fur salon was so afraid of poverty that Carol's refusal to go back to work drove him to kill. His need to feel important had previously driven him to lie to others about his education; though he had had less than one year at a small state college, he told others that he had attended Brown University on a football scholarship.

Charles hasn't talked ... except in the statement he made by killing himself. And his family has closed ranks.

The Mind of a Killer

For the most part, all we really know about any killer's emotions, upbringing, and reasons for destroying other people's lives is what he or she tells us. If, like Richard Ramirez, the "Nightstalker" who kept Los Angeles in terror throughout six months of 1985, they choose to say little except eye-catching, enigmatic phrases that make headlines, we can only go with our own speculation. Ramirez painted pentagrams on the walls in some houses he invaded, and he proclaimed in court that Satan would protect him. Otherwise, the Nightstalker said little.

Even if killers choose to talk, as Richard Speck did with Dr. Marvin Ziporyn, or Charles Starkweather with Dr. James Reinhardt, or Ted Bundy with Stephen Michaud and Hugh Aynesworth, we still know only what they choose to tell us.

Dr. Samuel Yochelson, a psychiatrist who gave up a lucrative private practice to study the criminal mind at St. Elizabeth's Hospital in Washington, D.C., expected to learn that the childhoods of the incarcerated men had driven them to crime and that coming to understand their pasts, the criminals could then rise above them. Instead, he quickly discovered that most criminals, learning the effect of their pasts on them, just used the knowledge to gain sympathy for their sad plights.

"Most criminals," he wrote in *The Criminal Personality*, "are cognizant of society's current way of thinking; even those who are untutored quickly pick up the prevailing views. They use life's adversities, sociologic or psychologic, to justify their criminal activity."

Almost two-thirds of the murderers discussed in this book were criminals first, before they became murderers.

Jack Graham got money by fiddling insurance claims before he blew up the airplane carrying his mother. Charles Manson spent most of his life in prison for various crimes. Albert DeSalvo was arrested for breaking and entering long before he killed his first woman. Ted Bundy furnished his apartments with high-quality stolen goods that gave him the setting of a man of taste and wealth, though he rarely took his numerous victims there. Even young suburbanite Chuck Riley was an adept shoplifter at a young age.

Other killers kill once and only once. They are generally noncriminal people whose frustration level reaches a point where they can no longer contain it and something must burst out, usually violence. That's the instant that Dr. Ziporyn calls the "moment when the brakes go." This type of killer usually finds his victim in the confines of personal relationships. Steven Steinberg killed his wife, and Dan White killed the men whom he held responsible for taking away his future and his vision of himself. Those relatively few women who kill are much, much more likely to be found killing people they know well than strangers. Only two women killers are to be found in this book, and they did the deed together.

Rarely are the hidden motivations the ones that police pursue or that prosecutors use to paint horror pictures that will cause a jury to send defendants to prison. Not that the revelation of hidden motivations in court will free killers. It did so, unusually enough, in the case of Steven Steinberg. More likely, it can, as in the case of Dan White, killer of the mayor of San Francisco, help a jury change its verdict from guilty of first-degree murder to guilty of voluntary manslaughter, a change that mitigates the punishment to be meted out. But, as in the case of the serial killers or mass murderers, it merely helps to explain for the satisfaction of an interested public. That same public would not allow a man to be freed who has murdered woman after woman or youth after youth, even if he were proved to be not responsible for his actions by reason of the hidden motivations that controlled his killing.

The Unanswerable "Why"

Beneath the superficial trigger, beneath the killer's hidden motivations that are the major instigators of murder, beneath the abuse, the rejection, the alcoholic blackouts, there is another "why," the fundamental one. Why, if two people are raised in virtually identical situations of poverty, abuse, abandonment, or compulsiveness, does one become a psychopath and a potential killer and the other work past his deprivations and become an average working citizen, albeit perhaps "normally" neurotic? Why does one woman with a totally inadequate sense of self reach out and kill someone, while another, raised in the same horror, becomes a victim of unending abuse, or a third strive to raise a normal, productive family?

This is the unanswerable "why."

As Virginia Adams wrote in a *Time* magazine essay in 1972: "The impulse to murder seems to be universal, but the reasons that men and women yield to it are as varied and mysterious as human history."

For generations, psychiatrists and the general public have avidly embraced the theory that something in a murderer's childhood environment provided the difference between the killer and the nonkiller. Even Dr. Yochelson, who did incredible work on analyzing the differences in thinking patterns between the criminal mind and the noncriminal, never got past the bottommost question: how did that difference in thinking arise?

This book is not going to attempt to answer the unanswerable "why." The shadows of my own early upbringing urge me to propose the existence of inherent, inexplicable evil in some people. But even that begs the issue, because, like a three-year-old who has just discovered how to drive a parent nuts with the question "why?", we then have to ask: why should that evil exist in one person and not another? That is the province of the theologian or the philosopher.

All we can do is try to understand, as far as we are able.

PART I

DOMINATION

THE KILLER PAIRS

The ultimate in the domination of one person over another is involving him or her in the ultimate crime, murder. For those people who feel as if they are nothing unless they are in control of whatever situation they find themselves in, domination in a love relationship confirms that they are important, that they are alive.

On the other side of the coin—or relationship—the fact that a person allows him- or herself to be dominated confirms that person's own worthlessness. For someone with virtually no self-esteem, there is a certain comfort in that confirmation.

In the following two chapters, we will meet fat, unlovely, and unloved Chuck Riley, who comes under the control of a dominating teenage "witch" and even kills for her. Jeannace Freeman decided that her lesbian lover's children were in the way, and Gertrude Jackson never questioned whether her toddlers should die.

Note that there are other pairs of killers covered in this book, but they do not appear to have experienced the domination of one over the other that is demonstrated here. Charles Starkweather had his fourteen-year-old girlfriend, Caril Ann Fugate, along with him on his murder spree, but she appears to have shared in the killing as enthusiastically as he. Kenneth Bianchi, one of the "Hillside Stranglers," killed for a major part of his deadly career with his cousin Angelo Buono. They egged each other on. If there was a subjugation involved, it was of Kenny Bianchi by the second personality within him, Steve.

I

Magical Enthrallment
Charles Riley

She's got control of my heart, mind, soul, all of me. I do all she says.

Charles Riley

The fat boy who had never dated, or even had many friends except those he bought by dealing drugs, was a compulsive overeater who failed at controlling his weight . . . until the first girl who responded to him urged him to diet. He did that for her. Then he began to steal for her. And finally he killed her parents for her . . . but then, he had no alternative: she controlled him—she was a witch.

From his earliest school years, Chuck Riley of Terra Linda, in Marin County, north of San Francisco, was laughed at by his peers for being fat, so he sought other ways to gain recognition, offsetting the frequent humiliations he experienced. Guns made him feel particularly good, and he practiced his marksmanship so much that he became a sure shot with both pellet guns, pistols, and rifles. The kids in the neighborhood admired his skill, just as their parents admired the fact that he was frequently named "carrier of the month" for the newspaper he delivered until he was seventeen. What those parents didn't know was that "Rocko"—the nickname that some friends managed to convert from the less innocuous "Boulder," given him for his size—was also a shoplifter and thief.

Oddly enough, it was his weight that eventually showed Chuck a way to get recognition from his peers. When a doctor put him on Dexedrine to help him lose weight, he discovered quite quickly that, while it didn't affect his weight very much, it helped him to feel "up" and confident. Until that time, he had stayed away from the pot-smoking scene. However, realizing that his dependence on the Dexedrine made him an addict anyway, he figured that he might as well join the other kids. It wasn't in Chuck Riley to be halfhearted about anything, though, and he joined them with a vengeance. First he smoked occasionally, then he became a heavy, daily smoker, and finally he started dealing in marijuana on a small level. When he discovered that his peers sought him out—almost as if they were friends instead of customers—he expanded his business so that he was dealing in hundreds of dollars' worth of marijuana and other drugs each week.

In the same way, Chuck regularly fell head over heels in fantasized love with girls he knew, but they never returned his attention, except when they wanted to buy. They were all into drugs—marijuana, cocaine, LSD, whatever they could get, and they used it at all times, even during breaks and lunch hour at school.

Chuck Riley quit school before graduating, but he didn't leave its environs because that's where his customers were. He grew a mustache and small beard in order to look older and started selling vacuum cleaners part time. But it was at the high school that he met Marlene Olive in the autumn of 1974.

Marlene

Marlene was a sexually precocious fifteen-year-old drug-user who had been raised in South America and only recently arrived in the area. Failing to fit immediately into the suburban California teen scene and feeling terribly isolated, she sought ways to make herself significant to the other kids. She shoplifted, joined the others in drugs . . . and began to delve into the occult.

The day Chuck first saw the voluptuous young blonde she was lying in a fetal position under a tree in the school grounds, spaced out on her first acid trip, one for which her "friends" had given her double the usual dosage of LSD. Chuck sat beside Marlene on the grass and helped the girl—who, unknown to her at that point, was already enthralling him—through the worst of her trip before she had to return to classes.

Marlene Olive had been adopted by Jim and Naomi

Olive of Norfolk, Virginia, when she was just hours old, the arrangements having been worked out with her teenage mother before the birth. The Olives then spent the next dozen or so years in South America, where Jim worked in petroleum sales. The lifestyle that their American income permitted there gave Marlene the certainty that she was supposed to be waited on hand and foot. It gave her mother Naomi the chance to quietly turn into a lazy, reclusive alcoholic, who isolated herself in mental illness and quickly lost all control over her daughter. Marlene grew to hate her mother and to expect whatever she asked for—attention and gifts—from her father. No matter what Marlene did wrong, Jim Olive paid for it by bringing her gifts.

When Jim's job ended, he, at fifty, had to find a new occupation. He bought a business franchise in northern California and took the family there. But neither his wife nor his daughter settled into the life. Each took her unhappiness out on the other with loud, abusive arguments, during which Marlene often bit into her own arm in anger, gradually building up extensive scar tissue there. Both Marlene and her mother compensated for their anger at each other by seeking a lot of attention from Jim, who failed to give it to either one while he was building his new business.

Marlene sought attention at her new school. She made up wild tales of her life in South America, claiming that she had been taught voodoo magic by the natives. She also took to dressing wildly and wearing massive quantities of makeup, so that both her parents began to call her "tramp." Her mother particularly began to make scathing references to Marlene turning into a "whore," just like her real mother. By age fourteen Marlene was involved in heavily sexual relationships with several different youths. One of them, a long-haired, would-be poet, introduced her to the occult, and she quickly immersed herself in the principles of black magic, with less than notable success. But magic became a major ingredient in her very active fantasy life.

There was no noticeable explosion when Marlene and Chuck met, except inside Chuck. He was convinced that love at first sight had struck him. The very next day, he returned to the school and asked Marlene to go to a movie with him. It was the first time that the introverted young man had ever asked a girl for a date. She was vaguely interested because he dealt drugs and looked older than her other friends. Although that appeal was offset by Riley's size, she accepted a double date for a movie. During the date, the four of them smoked pot continuously, and Marlene decided that she didn't like Chuck. What she did like, however, was his infatuation with her. From the start he was willing to do anything she asked in order to stay in her good graces. He was especially useful in supplying large quantities of drugs and other gifts.

One thing she asked was that he lose some of his massive weight. For the first time in his life, he had the incentive to diet and was successful. That should have strengthened his self-esteem, but whatever self Chuck Riley possessed was already lost in Marlene.

Throughout this period, Marlene dated the nineteen-year-old just occasionally, acquiescing to a date when the pressure he put on her reached a certain level, but she always took another person along. Chuck, who had never kissed the girl, watched in pain as she dated other boys and even became sexually involved with them. She was particularly fascinated by youths with bad reputations and even criminal records. One of them who swore he was into Satanism introduced her to tarot cards, which she began to "read" for her friends, with startling success at prediction.

Chuck stayed on the periphery of her crowd, continuing to send her gifts and to provide her and her friends with huge quantities of pot and cocaine. All she had to do to take advantage of his infatuation was to give him what she regarded as her special witch's "look," and he would hop to it. Whether she believed in the "look" or not, Chuck came to believe that she was using special powers on him. On one dramatic occasion she was sitting by him on the couch chatting, when she suddenly went into a "trance." She stared at nothing and mumbled for about fifteen minutes, while automatically writing strange symbols on a paper napkin. When she "came to," she identified the symbols as an alphabet used by witches. Chuck never doubted her for a moment.

It was while reading Anton Szandor LaVey's popular paperback *The Satanic Bible* that Marlene began to talk about the possibility of using her hated mother as a "human sacrifice." She claimed to be attending black masses held by a local witches coven—anything to make an impression on the other young people of the community. Some of the people she was trying particularly to impress were put off by the extent of her weirdness, and they started excluding her from their activities. It was only the insecure ones like Chuck Riley who continued to listen to Marlene, especially after she began to talk about killing her parents with more than the usual teenage "I-wish-my-parents-were-dead" type of talk.

It was an easy step, then, for her to start speculating on the best way to take care of the job. All her friends offered suggestions, not knowing that she was taking them seriously. Chuck was frequently included in these conversations because, after breaking up with another boy, she sought him out just to have a boyfriend around. He, of course, was ecstatic that his love was paying some attention to him. He even gathered the courage to make a physical pass at her, but she just shrugged it off, even though he knew she was regularly sleeping with other boys. The attention didn't last, however, because he made the mistake of introducing her to a young juvenile delinquent he knew, one who quickly captivated Marlene's attention while Chuck looked sadly on . . . again.

Marlene immediately pulled this new boyfriend, Ron Maddox, into her plans for killing her parents. As she would revise her plans, he would willingly—though never intending it for real—check out the details for her, as if really helping her. When she made the possible killings too real, though, he backed out, and she decided to run away instead.

On Marlene's sixteenth birthday, her mother found that

Marlene had stolen her credit card and played hooky from school. The pair had one of their increasingly devastating fights. When Chuck, who had been invited for a celebration dinner, arrived, Marlene conned him into taking her and her clothes to the house of a friend whom she knew would take her in.

Continually moving among friends in order to avoid her searching parents, Marlene held out for five days before giving up and going home. Ill with stomach pains that would later be found to be an ulcer, she readily agreed to try to get along better with her parents.

"Pussy Whipped"

Ron Maddox left town just ahead of the police, leaving Chuck Riley hoping that Marlene would finally turn to him. When he drove her on a brief trip, she did, indeed, turn to him. As they drove, she began to play with him sexually, and later that day, at age almost twenty, fat Chuck Riley had his first sexual experience.

To Chuck's astonishment and delight, Marlene seemed unable to get enough of him sexually. She would join him at motels or meet him at friends' houses. As she had controlled him emotionally since the day they met, she now controlled him sexually, too, delighting in humiliating him both when they were alone and in front of others. Every sexual fantasy that she had ever had she coerced him into performing with her, from group sex to posing out-of-doors for obscene photographs to performing cunnilingus on her in the midst of gatherings to masturbating together while on the telephone to violent sadomasochistic whippings. When she was angry with him, she often bit his arm so deeply through layers of clothing that it bled liberally. Each occasion added another scar to his skin, but he didn't mind. He didn't even mind when she carved her initials on his shoulder with a knife. He ignored his friends who pointed out that Marlene seemed to get more delight in embarrassing him than in loving him.

As a result of his complete immersion in Marlene, he neglected his friends, failed to be less than "honest" in his drug-dealing—something he had always taken pride in—and even gave up jobs when they interfered with his relationship with the sexy sixteen-year-old. All she had to do to get him to agree to anything was either to threaten to stop having sex with him or to give him the special witch's "look" that she had practiced so hard. To augment that look, she gave him a cheap bracelet she had acquired in South America that she told him would let her, as a witch, communicate with him. He believed that if he ever felt something in the wrist adorned by the bracelet—a tingling sensation or an itch—it meant that she was contacting him and he should telephone her at once.

Chuck, captivated even more fully, began to call her ten, twenty, thirty times a day. He even took to sleeping in outdoor telephone booths so that he could call her at any time during the night. And during endless conversations, she brewed more intricate plans for getting rid of her parents, plans that finally involved the cooperation of Chuck. Like all her other friends, he figured that Marlene was just "blowing off steam" and did not really mean to follow through with her plans.

Other plans they did follow through with, however. At Marlene's urging, the pair became highly adept at shoplifting, stealing hundreds of dollars' worth of fancy goods from the high-class stores of Marin County. When the two of them were finally arrested after several weeks of intense shoplifting, the security guards found well over a thousand dollars' worth of goods in Chuck's car. It was at that time that Marlene learned that in California she could, as a juvenile, be guilty of only two things: being beyond parental control and anything else. Even murder came under "anything else."

One probation officer later told Richard M. Levine, author of *Bad Blood*, Marlene's and Chuck's story: "The kids here [at the Marin County juvenile home] are angry at their parents, not at society. And the parents are more concerned with what the neighbors will think than with improving the situation at home."

Marlene's arrest shook her up enough so that when she was returned home from juvenile hall, she even made an effort to get along with her mother. . . .

Chuck, awaiting trial as a first-time adult offender, was ordered to have nothing to do with Marlene.

She wrote him a note telling him that she wasn't going to see him anymore. "I feel only emptiness in me, and a prayer for you, my love. Please forgive me for everything." Chuck didn't believe that she truly meant to drop out of his life. But when he went to the Olives' house,

Jim Olive threw him out. The next time Chuck would see Marlene's father would be when he was killing him.

Believing that the love affair was truly over, Chuck tried to commit suicide, but he failed to take enough of the weird assortment of drugs he had on hand to do the job.

In the meantime, Marlene, unable to keep up her commitment to get along with her mother, had a fight with her that ended only when the girl threw a knife. When her father sided with her mother, Marlene added her father to the list of people she wanted to die. But as her father spent less and less time at home because of his business, Marlene, too, tried to commit suicide with drugs. That night, purged of the drugs at a hospital, she wrote in her book of poetry: "And although she was alive, / She knew she couldn't survive."

Chuck continued to phone Marlene at frequent intervals, although they didn't manage to get together as often as before. Because his biggest fear was that she would break off the relationship entirely, he couldn't say no when she asked him to help kill her parents. She regularly ordered him to bring along his revolver when meeting her for dates, though she did nothing with it but check that he had, indeed, followed her command. When he gave the gun to a friend as collateral for a loan, he took to carrying a sawed-off shotgun so that Marlene would not find him unarmed. When the police stopped his car for an out-of-date registration, the shotgun was found and the pair were arrested, again. Once again, Jim Olive blamed Chuck and prevented Marlene from seeing him.

But it didn't prevent her writing to him. She poured out all her thoughts on paper, as, in early June 1975, her original shoplifting charge was brought before the court. She received only a rebuke and a written order to refrain from seeing Charles Riley, who was blamed for her problems. During the next two weeks, Marlene found herself increasingly alone in her own home. Her hostile mother retreated into her mental-illness-and-alcohol-induced isolation, while her father concentrated on his business moves. Marlene's letters to Chuck, some of them never mailed, referred more and more to "when" her parents were dead and the two of them would be free to marry.

As far as Chuck was concerned, equally important as the letters from Marlene were the sensations he received over her witch's bracelet, which he never removed from his wrist. He was certain that he always knew when she was angry, wanting him, or loving him, purely by the signals he perceived in his wrist. When he telephoned, however, the conversations tended to center on how to destroy her parents. He began to think she was serious, as did her other friends. She had gone beyond her long-term fantasy into realistic planning.

Steps to Murder

Marlene's report card arrived, and Jim Olive told her that the grades were so poor that he was going to send her to a boarding school in the fall.

Her mother caught her having sex with another boy, promised not to tell her father, and then told him anyway. Jim Olive forbade her to see any boys.

Then, finally, the father of an acquaintance of Marlene's called Jim Olive to say that Marlene had bilked his daughter out of forty dollars, money with which Marlene had agreed to purchase drugs at a discount for the friend. Marlene found herself grounded for the entire summer after her father agreed to pay the bill.

On Saturday, June 21, Chuck began drugging early since he would be unable to see Marlene—he thought. When he felt the tingling in his wrist that told him to call her, he phoned in the middle of a particularly vicious fight between Marlene and her mother.

"Get your gun. We've got to kill that bitch today," Marlene said to him as Naomi stormed out of the room. Hearing Marlene threaten never to speak to him again if he failed to appear with a gun, Chuck promised that, somehow, he would. He knew he had no alternative.

Later, while in the process of trying to keep his promise, he phoned Marlene again and learned that she was trying to poison her mother, as she had tried once before, by putting Darvon capsules in her food, but she also asked, "Where do I hit my mom to kill her? How hard do I hit her?"

Obtaining his old pistol on the story that he had someone interested in buying it, Chuck, who was having to hitchhike because his car was dead, phoned Marlene and had her send another friend to pick him up. On the way, the friend kindly went into a store to purchase ammunition for Chuck's gun. All the errands were done under the influence of a good Saturday dose of acid.

When Chuck arrived at Marlene's house—surreptitiously

as usual—Marlene met him in the garden and told him that she was leaving with her father to pay back the forty dollars but that he should go on into the house. He was to kill Naomi while she was gone.

Still floating in a cloud of drugs, Chuck Riley crept into the Olive house and found a claw hammer that Marlene had left by the front door after using it to fix a shoe. She had had it in her hand when she earlier asked Chuck how hard she would need to hit her mother to kill her.

Chuck walked into the room that had been Marlene's bedroom the last time he was in the house and found Mrs. Olive lying down, asleep on the bed. He struck her with the hammer, again and again, once having to yank it out of her skull where it jammed into the bone. Horrible sucking breaths told him that she wasn't dead, so he got a knife from the kitchen and stabbed her, too.

Marlene's father came home just then, considerably earlier than Chuck had expected. Marlene lingered at the door, letting her father enter first. When he saw his wife lying in a pool of blood, struggling to breathe, he turned on Chuck. Finally using his pistol, even though it was still in the bag he had carried it in, Chuck fired again and again and again. When the pistol fell, empty, at his side, his own personal witch, Marlene, entered the room and held him in her arms.

For the next several days, Marlene and Chuck lingered in the house, trying to clean it up and turning Naomi's bedroom into a family room. During the night, they took the corpses to a public picnic area called China Camp. There, in a large firepit and more by luck than planning, they managed to burn the bodies completely. They broke up the bones so that only tiny shards remained, and they destroyed the bloody mattress and rugs in which they had carried the bodies.

Chuck was happy in the glow of Marlene's love and gratitude . . . until she began to tell friends exactly what had happened to her parents. When Chuck had to go to work on his first day at a new job, Marlene invited herself to a friend's house, saying that her parents were away and she wanted company. While they chatted, Marlene told the friend everything. The friend, though, had heard it all before as fantasy and didn't recognize the truth when she heard it.

The next day, Marlene invited Sharon Dillon—another friend of whom her parents would never have approved— and begged her help in cleaning up bloodstains. They spent the afternoon shopping with her mother's credit cards. When Chuck, exuberant about his new job, came over that night, the three of them indulged in group sex. They then spent the rest of that week shopping with the Olives' money, drinking, dining expensively, indulging in sex, and trying to create alibis.

The following Saturday, a week after the murder, Jim Olive's business partner finally got tired of trying to locate him and called the police about his mysterious absence. When they entered the Olive house, the officers began to see that something was very wrong. That night, they took Marlene in for questioning. During the next hours, she told many different stories, mostly contradictory and mostly untrue. She tried her witch's "look" on the policemen, but it failed to have the effect it had always had on Chuck.

Not until they picked up Sharon Dillon did they begin to get a glimmer of the real truth. Following Sharon's instructions, the police investigated the firepit and found fragments of human bones, probably male and female.

Chuck Riley was arrested at his new job for what came to be called the "Barbecue Murder." The bracelet Marlene had given him was taken away from him when he reached the jail. Readily breaking down and talking, he told the story of the previous weeks and days, affirming that he had killed the Olives because "Marlene told me to."

He fretted about the missing bracelet because he felt bereft without contact with his beloved Marlene. He made up for his inability to see her by writing great long screeds that described every emotion, every action, every thought he had during the day. One friend came to see him, a friend who asked how it all happened. Chuck replied, "Marlene's a witch. She's got me under some kind of spell. She set the whole thing up and I carried it out." He confessed that it had all happened in a drug-induced haze.

Not long before his trial a kindly guard arranged for the bracelet Chuck yearned for to be given back to him. He hurriedly clamped it on his wrist; he relaxed and slept for the first time since it had been taken away from him.

Court psychiatrists who saw Chuck during the time

before his trial said, after reading some of Chuck's letters to Marlene, that he was in a devotion "akin to magical enthrallment." Another called their relationship "symbiotic," meaning that they fed on each other and that at least one partner (Chuck) was certain he could not survive without the other. But gradually, Marlene, who had never needed Chuck as much as he needed her, broke away and stopped writing.

In fact, she even stopped admitting to the authorities that she had played any role in the deaths of her parents at all. She hired an attorney who was willing to go for broke on a not-guilty plea, leaving Chuck to bear the burden alone. As Caril Ann Fugate had earlier said about Charles Starkweather, she claimed that during the week following the murder, Chuck had held her captive in the house.

Under the influence of hypnosis, Chuck, too, began to tell a different story, one in which he arrived at the house to find Naomi already dying from hammer blows inflicted by Marlene. But it made no difference to Marlene. California law required that any adult crime—be it simple theft or complex murder—committed by a juvenile be punished in the same way: confinement in a Youth Authority home until age twenty-one. Marlene would go free in four years.

At his trial in November 1975, Chuck's attorney tried to bring in the fact that he believed Marlene had control of his mind with her occult powers and that therefore he committed the murders in a time of diminished capacity—an inability to control his own actions. The defense tried desperately to get what Chuck had said under hypnosis admitted into court, but the judge refused to accept it, following a long history of inadmissibility of information learned through hypnosis. One psychiatrist testified that Chuck was certain he had experienced visitations from Satan. Chuck was seen to have not so much fallen in love as come under a "magic spell." It was a "grotesque caricature of love."

The jury didn't buy that defense, however. Charles Riley, twenty years old, was found guilty of two counts of murder in the first degree. As required by law, he was sentenced to death, although that sentence was later changed to life in prison by the U.S. Supreme Court decision on capital punishment.

Marlene Olive escaped from the juvenile facility. She went to New York City and, living one of the many fantasies she had enjoyed in years gone by, became a prostitute. After earning a lot of money and living high on the hog for some months, she was arrested and returned to California. Released in 1980, just before her twenty-first birthday, she dove heavily into the drug scene again. In 1981, she and Richard Levine, the author of *Bad Blood*, went together to see Chuck in prison and found that he had no interest in her.

The witchcraft had ended. The fatal link that had tied the ex-fat boy and his Marlene together had been severed.

2

"Whatever She Said, That Was It!"
Jeannace Freeman and Gertrude Jackson

> How can anyone rightfully blame me, at that time,
> nineteen years old; the mother, thirty-seven! I was
> still a child in many ways myself!
> > Jeannace Freeman in an open letter
> > to the people of Oregon

The two came together, one with a deep need to domi-
nate, the other with a need to be dominated. And the two
lesbian lovers agreed: the children were in the way. So
Jeannace Freeman and Gertrude Jackson killed Gertrude's
six-year-old son and four-year-old daughter. Jackson,
twice the age of her lover, never questioned that that was
the way it should be—after all, Jeannace, the dominant
one, had spoken.

Jeannace's Story
Jeannace June Freeman was born on a central Oregon

ranch in 1941, the sixth child of a large family. Soon after she was born, her parents were divorced because of her father's alcoholism, leaving her mother to support the many children as best she could by working long hours as a nurse. Somehow, she met a man, Clyde M. Whitcraft, who was willing to take on the large family, and she soon remarried. Whitcraft, a brickmason, had previously been convicted of rape.

Whitcraft did not stay around long, however, and Jeannace's mother indulged a habit of bringing men home whenever she felt like it. One of them, drunk after a dance, raped little Jeannace when she was four years old. "He hurt me awfully bad," she later told a school counselor. "I didn't tell my mother but she found out and she gave me a licking."

It's likely that the child called Jean was raped a number of times, probably by more than one man. In the letter she wrote to the people of Oregon in 1974, she said that the events "didn't twist my mind, except in the sense that I don't care for men. I did say men, not boys! In other words, when it comes to making love, I prefer women. Why? Because my body was brutally torn up when I was raped!"

Perhaps it was then that she acquired a determination, a need, to never again be subject to someone else; she needed to be the one in charge.

Things didn't get better as her mother changed men; the family just changed its locale, gradually moving from place to place, with Jeannace getting little education except in the ways of drunkenness and sex. Her mother seemed to take some delight in bragging to Jean and the other children about her sexual conquests, and often Jeannace would come home to find her mother having sex in the living room of their apartment or house. It was usually Jeannace who then took care of the new children who came along, and who worked at preparing meals for the family.

Jean was twelve when her mother moved the family to the university city of Eugene. There a school counselor who worked with the girl remembered for an *Oregon Journal* reporter years later: "Though her face was prettier than average, it also impressed me as a face that had known trouble way beyond that of a normal twelve-year-old." It was in Eugene that year that she met, at a fast-food place, a college girl from Spain. The exotic-seeming student gradually introduced the immature child to lesbian love, a whole new and welcome experience after the education Jean had had with heterosexual activity.

At fourteen, Jeannace, announcing herself as a lesbian, went to live in a county juvenile home at the request of her mother, who was at a financial low and wanted her child made a ward of the court. Jeannace stayed there only a few months but in that time acquired a passionate attachment to and dependence on her counselor and a school official. The counselor recognized that the girl was completely incapable of dealing with other girls and boys of her own age. In fact, most of her dealings with them involved fights and resulted in bruises, which she took delight in showing off. The counselor wrote, "I feel that Jean is much in need of psychiatric help. I feel this is an emergency situation.''

The help wasn't forthcoming, although three months later the home did send her to a psychiatrist whose report would figure in her murder trial four years later. In talking with Jean, he learned that she was fully aware of her desire to have been a boy. Except for the possibility of being a mother, she saw only disadvantages in being a girl and was trying her hardest to overcome them by not being one. However, she displayed skill and caring in tending younger children, and among her few good grades in school were those for the homemaking courses. However, he also noted, ''Her seductive mannerisms preclude the possibility of working with a male therapist.''

And there the matter sat because no government body was willing to pay the cost of psychiatric help for young Jean. Instead, not knowing what to do with her and finding her disturbingly ''rebellious,'' the county let her quit high school and work caring for the smaller children in one of the houses making up the juvenile institution. Then, although she had never been in trouble with the law, the county, not knowing what else to do with her, sent Jeannace Freeman to a home for juvenile delinquents.

Whatever tendencies to conform that Jeannace might have had were trashed at the home. She was continually in trouble with the school authorities—for increasing misbehavior, for not applying herself to school work, for sexually pursuing any other female who might be available, and for being a ''general nuisance.'' It was there that she managed to have her body tattooed in many different places, including the letters H-A-T-E on her fingers. It was also while at that school that her ex-stepfather (he and her mother were divorced in 1955, though they continued to live together on and off) was tried for contributing to the delinquency of a minor, a fourteen-year-old girl who was a friend of Jeannace's. He was placed on probation for five years.

Jeannace was released from the school when she was sixteen, with little attention on the part of officials as to where she would go from there. The girl who most frequently wore boy's blue jeans and cowboy boots lived with various relatives in Klamath Falls for some months, but did not complete high school. Returning to Eugene in 1961, she soon took a job babysitting for Gertrude Jackson.

Gertrude's Story

Gertrude Mae Clark, the second of two daughters, was born in 1927 in The Dalles, Oregon, to a railroad trainman who could not deal with life. He committed suicide in 1932, when Gertrude was only five years old. Her mother, trying to deal with life in her own way, just as Jeannace's mother would have to do, took her daughters to Portland, where she became a fixture waiting tables in the daytime and drinking in the bars at night.

Gertrude and her school work received no attention from her mother, or, ultimately, from Gertrude herself. She was held back two different times in grade school, as much for truancy as for bad work when she was there. Her sister, five years older, turned to prostitution as a teenager and quickly saw the value of her younger sister. Gertrude experienced her first sexual intercourse when she was still in grade school, though she was probably twelve or thirteen. An older man introduced her to sex, and she was soon regularly serving as a special treat that her sister would serve up to men who would pay extra for the youngster. It's unlikely that Gertrude had much choice in the matter.

When she was fifteen, Gertrude found a sailor she met to be special—so special that she ran away with him to Seattle. But if she had some sort of a permanent relationship in mind, he didn't, and he abandoned her in the strange city. When she was finally located by her family, she was sent back home, where she became a ward of the county and was sent to an industrial school. Her sister Ruby, who was also sent to the school, married a man in order to get out. Agreeing to free Gertrude from the school, too, he became responsible for her.

An attractive, virile Mexican farm laborer caught Gertrude's attention, and immediately after her eighteenth birthday she married Gregorio Nunez. However, it wasn't really marriage he had in mind, just an opportunity for U.S. citizenship. He regularly beat the girl and—willingly or unwillingly—she found herself being given to his friends. One of them fathered a child on Gertrude, a boy named Manuel, who went with Gregorio when he abandoned the mother.

Now on her own, Gertrude moved around Oregon and California as the will took her, probably working as a prostitute when she found no other means at hand to pay her bills. In 1955, she settled down in Oakland, California, with a black construction worker, Dempsey Otis Jackson. He, too, beat her regularly and forced her to keep working to pay for his narcotics addiction, even after giving birth to two children, a boy named Larry and a girl, Martha.

The birth of the children brought new problems—those of prejudice, because the children were obviously of mixed parentage, and some day-care centers refused to keep them. It was hard enough to pay for day care anyway on a salary of forty-five dollars a week as a shirt-presser in a laundry. And Gertrude suffered the additional problem of all women who choose to stay in a situation in which they will be beaten—progressive shattering of all self-respect and gradual growth of the belief that they deserve what they get.

In 1960, however, Gertrude gathered the courage to leave Jackson, though she continued to use his name, and she returned to Eugene, Oregon. Because managing her family's lives became too difficult for her, she started to make arrangements to put the children in a foster home, but at the last moment she could not do it. Instead, she kept on working in laundries and hiring babysitters for as little money as she could get away with.

In February 1961, Gertrude met slender, pert Jeannace Freeman.

The Children Were in the Way

And so Gertrude—thirty-three years old, with an attractively rounded body and curly hair—and Jeannace—

nineteen, thin and flat-chested, with her brown hair in a boyish cut—came together at a party in early 1961, and were immediately attracted to each other, despite their age difference—or perhaps because of that age difference. Jeannace currently had a girlfriend, Letha June Little, who apparently did not complain when their twosome became a triangle. Gertrude, seeing a tenderness that she had never found in men, readily became Jean's new lover.

First the two were lovers, then they worked out an arrangement by which Jeannace, who needed a job, became the paid babysitter for six-year-old Larry and four-year-old Marty, while Gertrude worked at the laundry, earning a pittance of a living. Somehow Jeannace talked Gertrude into quitting her job and, with Letha June, the pair took the children south into California, hoping to start new lives in Berkeley or Oakland.

They found an apartment in Oakland, but Jeannace frequently grumbled about how hard it was to carry on a love affair in the presence of two small, lively, inquisitive children. She frequently sent the kids out to play and otherwise ignored them. Gertrude acquiesced in trying to get rid of her children and found a foster home for them, but they were returned to her when they were found to be part Negro.

And so the talk turned to getting rid of the children. Neither Jeannace nor Gertrude had ever learned that she as an individual had any value, so neither placed any value on the lives of the children. Instead of giving them away or abandoning them somewhere they might be found, they chose to eliminate them forever. Jeannace said she knew the perfect place.

The pair drove back up into central Oregon and, in the darkness of predawn on May 11, 1961, they entered Peter Skene Ogden State Park and stopped at Crooked River Canyon, a dramatically deep gorge. The two children were asleep in the backseat of the car. Jeannace, who may or may not have sent Gertrude away for a few minutes, struck the six-year-old boy over the head. The later autopsy showed that he was dead from that blow before she proceeded to choke him and to mutilate his genital area with a tire iron, hoping to make it look as if he had been raped by a man. When Gertrude returned, Jeannace threw the naked little body down into the gorge, a straight drop of over three hundred and sixty feet, the equivalent of a twenty-seven-story building. Little four-year-old Martha was also mutilated but was still alive when her mother threw her, also naked, into the gorge after her brother.

The women cleaned themselves up and went to visit Jeannace's stepfather in Culver and even blithely went fishing in the same river by which the children's bodies lay. He noticed that the children were not with them but accepted their statement that the kids had been put in a foster home. The women picked up Letha, the third member of their triangle, and then drove back south, throwing the children's clothing out of the car window along the way. In Oakland, they sold the old Mercury they had been driving and moved out of the apartment so that if there were problems, they would avoid being caught.

The bodies of the two little ones—which looked like tiny broken dolls from up on the roadway—were found the following day by hikers. The mothers of Oregon trembled with fear that a child killer was loose in the area. The bodies were not identified until three days later, when Jeannace's ex-stepfather told police that the pictures in the newspaper looked like Gertrude Jackson's children. He was able to give police the license number of their car, which was spotted in a used-car lot in California. The women were arrested in Oakland when they made the mistake of returning to their first apartment for some things they had left behind.

Whatever relationship the two had had, brief though it was, was gone instantly. Tough, boyish Jeannace Freeman refused to admit that she had done wrong. She said that Gertrude had told her to stop the car and had beaten the children and thrown them into the gorge, threatening her young lover with a similar death if she ever told on her. Gertrude, on the other hand, immediately broke into tears. She said that she had left the children with Jean for a few minutes and come back to find her son dead. Then, feeling that Martha should not live without her brother, she had thrown the girl into the gorge, too.

Jeannace took no blame for the killings—until 1974, when she wrote in her open letter to the people of Oregon:

"Would it interest anyone to know that I meant to kill [the boy's] mother, only she pushed him in the way; and he caught the blow that I meant for her? Can you understand how I did panic? . . . What kind of mother was she, that she could push her own flesh and blood in the way of a blow meant for her? And what kind of a mother would deliberately throw her own daughter into that same canyon . . . ?'' She added that Gertrude, knowing Jeannace's violent temper, deliberately provoked her to blows, planning to make her kill the children.

Gertrude Nunez Jackson pleaded guilty to the death of her daughter and was sentenced to life in prison. Because the courts and parole board held that she had been under the subjugation of Jeannace at the time she killed her daughter, she was released after only seven years.

At her trial in September 1961 for the murder of six-year-old Larry, Jeannace June Freeman, wearing skirts and with her hair in curls, pleaded not guilty. However, she was found to be guilty and was sentenced to die, the first woman in Oregon history to be given the death penalty.

Thomas E. Gaddis, a psychiatrist who felt that the women should have received equal sentences, wrote: ''Surely no 'mom' would kill her own children like this. That goes against motherhood. So this mother must have been dominated, hypnotized, forced to do it. Therefore only one person was really guilty—the 'man-like' person in this revolting alliance. So this mother confesses, says she's sorry, and lays the blame on her young friend.'' He added, ''It is as plausible to believe that the Freeman girl acceded to the 'feminine' imploring of Mrs. Nunez to get rid of the children, as it is to believe that Mrs. Nunez acceded to the 'masculine' demanding of the Freeman girl.''

Jeannace lived on Death Row for three years, until the residents of Oregon voted to abolish capital punishment. At first she was continuous trouble in prison, even starting a riot at one time by being placed in isolation after belligerently keeping her radio turned too loudly. The maturing woman gradually settled down. She even had her tattoos removed, though she has born the scars since.

Paroled in 1983 after spending twenty-two years locked up, Jeannace was returned to prison six months later after she was found to be living in Washington with a woman and her minor children—strictly prohibited by the terms of her parole. She was finally released for good in 1985 at age forty-four.

In 1974 Jeannace Freeman, hoping to be paroled, wrote her letter to the people to Oregon, which was published in the newspapers. She concluded it: ''What do you think? Can you truthfully say that I deserve to be kept locked up longer? Or do you even care? Did anyone ever really care? When it comes to caring, who cared when I was so brutally abused? My mother, yes, but she wasn't there at the time or it wouldn't have happened!

''In closing, I remain, ME!''

PART II

EXPLOSION OF RAGE
Driven To Murder

The addition of one small frustration to an already strained situation may trigger aggressive behavior. This theory may help to explain excessively violent responses to apparently trivial incidents.
—From the Report of the National Commission on the Causes and Prevention of Violence

Most of us lose our "cool" sometimes, when the stresses of living just become too much for us for a few minutes. We rant and rave. Perhaps we strike out blindly, not even realizing what we're doing, even though normally we would not consider the use of physical force.

A few of us—fortunately, only a few—kill someone while we're in such a state. We are driven to the use of violence by the "one small frustration" mentioned above. Legally, such a state is called *diminished capacity*. For brief minutes, even seconds, we lose the capacity to tell right from wrong, to use our intellect to stop us from doing the wrong thing.

Albert Berry was a Californian who married an Israeli woman named Rachel. Berry, always jealous and fearful in his relationships with women, tried to choke her one night when he was convinced that she was seeing another man. She spent three days in the hospital, filing a criminal complaint against him while she was there. On her return to their apartment, Albert was lying in wait, telephone cord in hand. When he said that he might kill her, Rachel began to scream. That scream drove him over the edge and he strangled her in earnest.

Albert Berry's defense team brought in psychiatrist Martin Blinder. He determined that Rachel had, in fact, wanted to commit suicide but had not had the courage to carry out the deed. Instead, she had used her cupidity— and Albert's jealousy—to force Albert into killing her, which he did, during a period of *dissociative reaction*, which Blinder defined in another trial as "the splitting off of some or all elements of consciousness, control and recollection."

The jury still found Albert guilty of murder in the first degree, but the California supreme court, on reviewing the case, called for a second trial and printed what came to be called Blinder's "psychiatric autopsy" of Rachel, though the court did not comment on his report. Before the second trial could be held, Albert Berry changed his plea to guilty, but Blinder's technique of psychiatric autopsy of the victim had made its way into the California courts.

Blinder would use similar techniques in the psychiatric defense of two other killers who are described in the following pages: Steven Steinberg, an Arizona business-man who killed his "nagging" wife, and Supervisor Dan White of San Francisco, who, his frustration driven past its limits by vast quantities of sugary junk foods, killed the mayor and another supervisor.

But let's start with Italian immigrant Frank Archina, who only wanted the chance to marry the girl he loved . . .

3

"We Made Him Do It"
Frank Archina

> He came [to America] for a religious marriage and
> found himself a slave.
> Dr. J. P. Hilton, Denver psychiatrist

Day by day, month by month, Italian immigrant Francesco
Archina's father-in-law forced him to put off the church
wedding that would let him be truly married to his
American wife. Day by day, month by month, Frank
Archina acquiesced in the delay that kept him from the
bed of the woman to whom he was already married in a
civil ceremony... until one day his rage erupted and
murder was the result.

Young Francesco Archina, his brother Luigi, and a
third Archina son were just three more residents of the
rather poor farm town of Siderno Marino, Italy. They

were luckier than some in that they had each other, unluckier than others in that their father was dead and their mother was not always able to keep food on the table. Francesco had the additional problem of being epileptic, sometimes having seizures that caused him to lose control of himself and then forget what he did during the attacks.

Francesco was forced to leave school at age fourteen and go to work. He had several jobs at menial labor before becoming a sharecropper with his brother Luigi. But then his luck changed, or so it certainly seemed to his friends who saw Francesco and Luigi get introduced to Rose and Mary Macri, two American-born Italian girls whose family had returned to Italy before World War II. Soon the two brothers became betrothed to the two sisters, and plans were made for them to marry in a civil ceremony so that they could emigrate to America.

The Macri family had gone to America from Siderno in the early 1930s, settling in the Denver, Colorado, area. Frank Macri and his wife Elizabeth did well in America, but after their sons, Steve and Frank, Jr., and their daughters, Mary and Rose, were born, they decided to return to Italy. The war made Frank, Sr., realize the mistake he had made, and he began to make plans to take his family back to America when the war was over. However, he wanted to be sure that his girls would have good Catholic Italian boys to marry. His sister introduced the young Archina boys, just entering their teens, to Macri, who found the earnest, hard-working youths to be suitable prospective husbands for his beloved daughters.

The two couples were betrothed and went on with the serious business of growing up in a world at war. The girls were not given much opportunity to express their own opinions about the future marriages, though Rose found the tall, dark-haired Frank increasingly attractive.

In 1950, the senior Macri and his sons returned to the United States to establish a home in the Denver area, while Mrs. Macri stayed with the girls so that they could get better acquainted with their prospective husbands. Finally, in June 1951, the two brothers, now nineteen and twenty, and two sisters, seventeen and eighteen, were married in a civil ceremony. Francesco—now calling himself Frank—the younger, married the younger girl, Rosinne Joanne Macri—called Rose. Luigi—often called Gene—married Mary, the older sister. This ceremony, however, meant nothing to either strictly Catholic family except as a legal means of getting the boys into the United States. They would not really be married until they were married in the church.

Before he left for America, Frank Macri, Sr., had exacted a promise from the boys that they would make no attempt to consummate their marriages until after a religious ceremony, which would not be held until all of them were in America. The boys, good Catholics, readily agreed. Besides, Mrs. Macri and her sister-in-law were there to keep a very stern eye on the two couples to make sure that there was no hanky-panky. But Frank Archina could hope, and look forward to the day that the pretty, petite Rose would truly be his.

Mrs. Macri and the young not-quite-wives left for

America a few months after the civil ceremony. Frank and Luigi finished cleaning up their responsibilities in Siderno and sailed to the United States in January 1953. They went right on to Denver, where they moved into bedrooms on the second floor of the house that Frank Macri, Sr., had prepared for the family. Macri, who suffered from heart trouble and was unable to work, made his major task keeping his daughters tucked safely away in their own bedrooms, out of reach of the young Italians.

Frank and Luigi, unable to speak any English, took jobs as laborers but promptly signed up for English-language classes. As they saw the girls scurrying from the bathroom to their own bedroom each evening, they started to ask when the religious ceremony that would make the girls their wives would be held. Their father-in-law, quite reasonably, he thought, requested that they be secure in their work and have some money put away to pay for the elaborate ceremony before they set the actual wedding date. The boys agreed, albeit reluctantly. They found it difficult, night after night, to leave their alluring young wives after dinner and pretend that they were not living on the same floor of the same house. It was especially hard to leave them after an evening at the movies, which the four of them enjoyed as often as possible because they could touch each other in ways that they couldn't when their father was around.

But save they did, working day by day at their jobs in a local brickyard, until the boys felt they had saved enough for a date to be set for the elaborate religious ceremony the family demanded. Then Macri shocked them by demanding that they save enough to set up their own apartments, so his daughters would have homes of their own. Angrily the two argued, and then agreed— because they had no choice. It was up to the senior Macri, as a traditional Italian father, to decree when his girls could be married.

However, night after night, Frank found it harder and harder to ignore the sexual arousal he felt in the presence of the girl who was not yet his wife, and to go to his celibate room. The tension built, especially when Rose, who worked in a candy factory, would not come home in the evening after work and he didn't know where she was. He grew increasingly jealous at the thought that since they weren't truly married yet—at least in their own eyes—she might be looking at other eligible young men. In her teenage willfulness, she often refused to tell Frank where she was going or who she had been with. When he did learn that she often went out to supper and perhaps the movies with friends from work, he didn't like that much better.

And so the tension grew, as evidenced by the fact that Frank, previously a solidly built young man, lost sixty pounds during this period.

Frank had agreed to wait, but he didn't like it, and he brought the subject of their marriage up as often as he dared, hoping that the stern patriarch would ease his requirements. Instead, Macri taunted the boys and talked about the beautiful, *expensive* furniture he would expect his daughters to have in the apartments his sons-in-law would provide after the fancy wedding ceremony they must pay for. The tension tautened.

On Saturday night, January 23, 1954, Frank, according to his brother, experienced an epileptic episode, which left him crying the entire night. The next morning he went to see a doctor for an injection. After church that day, the family, including the not-quite-sons-in-law, finished lunch. Then, as usual, the women went into the kitchen to clean up while the men relaxed in the living room. Frank again brought up the subject of the long-awaited church wedding, hoping that by some miracle Macri would have changed his mind. Frank brought into the argument the difficulty he had watching his "wife" being free to go out and about on her own.

"You don't know how to correct your children," Archina screamed at his father-in-law.

"I do know because I was born before you," rejoined Macri, enraged at the criticism.

Frank Macri, Jr., who was also present, shook Archina by the shoulders, shouting for him to "behave!" Archina, suddenly enraged by all the waiting and apparently suffering an epileptic fit, punched Macri in the head. When the older man fell, Archina kicked him in the stomach and then tore upstairs to his bedroom to get one of the shotguns he used for hunting.

Rose, Archina's wife-fiancée, screamed, "He's going to get his gun!" The shaking Macri leaped to his feet and grabbed his own gun from a closet. He drove his wife and daughters, who had appeared from the kitchen, into a bedroom closet where they would be out of the way of any fight. Archina came down the stairs firing, his first blast immediately killing Frank Macri, Sr., as he emerged from the downstairs bedroom. Another blast seriously wounded Frank, Jr.

Still possessed by the rage, Archina marched into the bedroom and yanked open the closet door. He saw Mrs. Macri kneeling on the floor in front of him, pleading, "Please don't shoot us!" But he fired twice, mere inches from her mouth, virtually blowing her head away.

His wife and sister-in-law cowered back into the closet while he reloaded his shotgun and then fired two more shots at Mary. One load entered her side, and the other tore away her arm. Finally he faced Rose, the girl he wanted so much to be his wife. She was certain that she was about to die when he placed the muzzle at her neck and pulled the trigger again. But the shotgun failed to fire because he had inserted a 20-gauge shell in a 16-gauge shotgun.

The futile click brought Frank Archina out of his blackout. He drove the butt of the shotgun through a window, jumped out, and disappeared down the street. The police found him sometime later in a nearby tavern. The bartender told the police that the young Italian had been sitting alone in a booth, staring into space, for long minutes at a time. Frank Archina, the man who only wanted to be a real husband, was arrested for murder. He had no memory of what he had done.

Frank Macri, Sr., had died instantly, as had his wife. Frank, Jr., who had tried to protect his father, died several hours later. Mary remained in critical condition until her death less than three weeks later. Of the Macri family, only Rose and her younger brother Steve, who had been outside washing his car when the fight began, survived.

Frank Archina was tried only for the murder of Mrs. Elizabeth Macri, since that death was the most straight-forwardly witnessed and did not involve the possibility of self-defense. Ironically, the fact that the Archina marriage had never been consummated, which was the cause of the problem, allowed Rose to testify against her husband, according to Colorado law. If they had ever slept togeth-er, the only living witness to the entire death scene would not have been able to testify in court. Not that the nineteen-year-old had any intention of withholding her testimony; Rose wanted desperately to see Frank found guilty. She testified that he was jealous of her seeing anyone else and tried to keep her home, never letting her enjoy life. She also claimed that Frank himself had chosen not to hurry into the religious ceremony, that Frank Macri's quarrel with him had been because he was refusing to marry Rose. She also insisted that Frank had agreed to the marriage just as a means of entering the United States. The wife-that-never-was filed for an an-nulment soon after the murders.

Archina's attorneys entered a plea of not guilty by reason of insanity. The trial that began in August 1954 ended in a mistrial after one of the jurors became so ill that he could not continue. It was just the first in a series of both murder and sanity trials that would not settle

Frank Archina's future until 1963, nine and a half years after the murders occurred.

At the beginning, all voices at the trial had to be translated into and from Italian because of Archina's inability to speak English, but he gradually learned the language while in prison.

The jury at the second trial found him guilty of murder and sentenced him to die, a sentence that was confirmed when a sanity trial found him sane on the word of two psychiatrists. Archina swore that Rose had lied throughout her testimony. Immediately after that finding, the young Italian's attorneys filed for a new trial, charging that Rose should not have been allowed to testify, as well as pointing out some other judicial errors.

The state supreme court reversed the verdict, primarily because the district attorney had made untrue statements to the jury and failed to prove other statements. They accepted the validity of Rose's testimony, saying that they did not believe that the Italian civil ceremony was binding. The court insisted that another trial be held. It took place in the summer of 1957.

Again Rose was permitted to testify, but this time Frank Archina's childhood physician was brought from Italy to testify about his epilepsy. Also at that trial was a surprise witness, Robert Koch, a schoolteacher neighbor of the Macris. He testified that on the afternoon of the murders he heard the noises and entered the Macri house before the police arrived but after Rose had run for help. He found Mary lying on the floor in her own blood and heard her whisper, "Don't let them hurt him. We made him do it. He wouldn't hurt me.'' Koch had never volunteered the information before because he didn't want to get into trouble for moving the bodies.

The prosecution tried to discredit this testimony on the basis that Koch had a record as a convicted felon (for the theft of a calf in 1948). In addition, Rose testified that Mary could say no more than ''How are you?'' in English.

The jury at this trial acquitted Frank Archina by reason of insanity, accepting the testimony of his childhood physician that he was under the sway of an epileptic fit during the murders. He was committed to the state hospital until such time as he was ''restored to reason.''

Ironically, this decision gave the United States government the ammunition it needed to send Archina back to Italy. At that time, one of the rules preventing the immigration of an individual into the U.S. was a history of epilepsy, so Frank Archina had lied on his application for immigrant status. As part of the negotiations, he agreed to let Rose's annulment go through.

In May 1958, Archina was declared sane, released from the hospital, and, in August, deported to his native Italy. He expected that he would finally go free, but he didn't know about the ancient Italian law that allowed Italian courts to try its citizens for crimes committed elsewhere, regardless of ''elsewhere's'' own court verdict. On his arrival in Rome, he was arrested and sent to prison again. This time he was found to have been sane and he was indicted for murder.

While he waited for that trial to take place, Rose's

annulment failed to go through and she finally pursued a legal divorce. It was granted in July 1960, for the best of all reasons: "He killed several members of my family and he threatened to kill me too."

The following year, using the transcript of the Denver trials as the primary evidence, the Roman court found Archina—again called "Francesco"—guilty of two murders, his mother-in-law and Mary, his sister-in-law, as well as the attempted murder of his wife. The killing of his father-in-law and brother-in-law was ignored because they had held weapons at the time, and so their deaths could be regarded as self-defense. He was sentenced to ten years in prison. In summer 1963, the court decided that all the time Archina had already spent in jail in the United States should be counted as part of the sentence, and he was released to begin life anew in the Italy he had left more than ten years before.

4

"I Didn't Know I Was Unhappy"
Steven Steinberg

> I don't remember actually killing her myself, but it is obvious what I did do. I just don't remember doing it.
>
> Steven Steinberg

They were the ideal couple when they married—young, attractive, with similar upbringings in close-knit, second-generation Jewish families, talented but with no arguments about the wife's job—she stayed at home, created a beautiful setting for their lives, and raised the children. But when she died fifteen years later from twenty-six blows of a long, sharp kitchen knife wielded by her husband, the defense psychiatrists showed that her own behavior, her desperate need for more and more money, had pressured Steven Steinberg into killing his wife. He was acquitted by the jury, because, in effect, "she deserved it."

* * *

Elana Joy Singer, at sixteen, was attracted to Steven F. Steinberg from the moment they met. Three years older, he had an air of "tough guy" about him that went well with his dark good looks, and even her parents found him appealing. They were willing to let him treat their home as his. After all, his had been disrupted when Steven was only twelve. He was roughhousing with his father, who keeled over with a massive heart attack. Elana's parents thought that the young man who still felt so guilty over the death of his father was in deep need of affection, and they were ready to give it to him.

Steve and Elana were married in May 1966 in a grand and expensive celebration that left Steve feeling defensive. He always made sure that people knew that his mother and stepfather had paid for part of the big bash. The pair lived fairly well from the start—dining out a lot, taking plush vacations, furnishing an apartment with nice things, quickly moving beyond most of the young married couples they knew, especially when pushed on by an ambitious Elana. They made an agreement early on: Steve would make the money and Elana would control it, which for her meant spending it.

During the next years, the couple appeared at first to be moving up in the world. They bought a small house in the Chicago suburbs, which Elana decorated with great skill. They had two daughters, whom Elana made sure had the best of everything.

But then they got bogged down. Steve couldn't seem to make the important career moves that he needed, despite the help of his father-in-law. He worked hard, and customers at the various stores where he worked liked him a lot. But strange things seemed to happen around him. Large amounts of money were taken from the cash registers where he worked, even at his own father-in-law's store, though Barney Singer never suspected that Steve might have had something to do with those disappearances. For what wasn't known by the others was the fact that Steve was gambling, apparently for the joy that Elana's face showed and the gestures of love she gave when he presented his winnings to her. After a while, he stopped telling her when he lost, because she managed to make him feel inadequate. When he didn't have the funds to pay his losses, he apparently got money where he could, though none of those mysterious thefts was ever charged to him.

In the mid-seventies, the entire Singer clan—first younger son Mitchell, then parents Barney and Edith Singer, and finally daughter Elana and her husband—moved to Arizona. Steve's mother, stepfather, and sister soon followed. Barney offered to start a new business in the Phoenix area with Steve as a partner, an opportunity Steve saw as one that would provide him with all the money he might need.

Their move to Arizona took them into an entirely different lifestyle, one in which only money counted—or, not even money, just the *appearance* of money. Elana's brother Mitch opened a chain of restaurants that became the "in" places to go for several years. Elana and Steve acquired some vicarious panache for being related to the Mitchell Singer who ran the "B. B. Singer" restaurants.

In fact, Steve took a job with Mitch after his and Barney's pool-and-patio store closed. The combination of the inexplicably large losses of cash and their far too relaxed approach to management forced Steve and his father-in-law to sell the store. What profit there was Elana took and put into certificates of deposit, CDs that Steve would try, time after time, to get away from her.

Steve went to work for Mitch, his brother-in-law, expecting to be made a partner and to have full access to the apparently large quantities of money that went through the restaurants. But he did not realize that Mitch did not really "own" the restaurants. As often happens in the restaurant business, he leased both the premises and the equipment, owning nothing but the name and his own ability to attract people. If the fad for the "in" restaurant changed, he had nothing to back it up. However, the new manager was very popular with the customers and appeared on the surface to be doing well, an appearance that Elana treasured and lived up to.

Beneath the surface, however, Steve was losing more and more at gambling. The banks that he went to were well aware of his success at the famed restaurants and were perfectly willing to lend him the money he required to keep on gambling, though that, of course, was not the official reason for the loans. Elana never knew about the loans, some of which were made in order to pay back others, creating a more and more fragile structure that was about to tumble. Steve worked hard all day, played poker and arranged bets in the evening, and partied with friends on weekends. The facade that everything was going well was very firm, especially because Elana put such pains into having her house in the luxurious subdivision of Scottsdale called McCormick Ranch looking just perfect, her children well dressed and properly behaved, and her parties known for their elegance.

But behind the scenes, the restaurant income was failing. Some bad decisions on Mitch's part, plus a lack of awareness that the popularity of the chain was falling off, led to him selling part of the business to some New York investors. When the newcomers demanded that Steve put in more days per week and give up some of the perquisites he had enjoyed, such as a Lincoln Mark II, he quit, without Elana's agreement. Steve started going to real-estate school at night. But the pressure from the banks and the "friend" who served as his bookie to pay old bets was getting to him. It was never made easier by Elana's fretful nagging about needing more money to meet their expenses.

The Unconscious Act

On Wednesday, May 27, 1981, two days before the couple's fifteenth anniversary, Steve collected his first unemployment check. That evening, he went to play in a softball game. He seemed kind of preoccupied, some other players thought. After the game, the atmosphere was sultry with an undelivered storm.

The Steinberg daughters were in bed; it was a school night, though the school year was almost over. Traci, the twelve-year-old, woke to the sound of her mother screaming. Hearing her shout for Traci and six-year-old Shawn,

Traci went running out into the hall, calling her mother's name. But her father screamed, "Shut your fucking door!" Later, in court, though she had never seen her father again and she refused to help him, Traci was unable to say aloud what he had said to her. Although she substituted the word "goddamn," she had already told an investigator the true, unfeeling term her father had used.

Traci ran back to her room and lay in bed quivering. But not for long.

Just after midnight, Steve called a female acquaintance, shouting, "Come over right away—right now!" But he did not identify himself, and she did not know Steve Steinberg well enough to recognize his voice. She never did understand why he called her.

A few minutes later, at 12:07, a call came into police headquarters and was tape recorded. Steve Steinberg's voice said, "My wife was just murdered, and they walked in the house, my God, please—I'm bleeding, I'm trying to stop the bleeding!" Then Traci's hysterical voice broke in: "This is his daughter, please hurry. I'm here, I'm Traci. I'm scared!"

The first police car arriving at the house was met by Steinberg. He was dressed in his bathrobe and was holding a towel around his hand. He shouted, "They killed my wife! There are two of them, they've gone, they went out the back door . . ."

The first sight that met the eyes of the appalled policemen as they entered the Steinbergs' bedroom was a massive pool of blood in the middle of the big bed.

Spatters of horrible dripping redness ruined Elana's meticulous decor. A dresser drawer was pulled open and some of her petite underpants lay on the floor. And by the side of the bed, leaning against the frame, was a very mutilated and very dead Elana Steinberg. She had been viciously stabbed over and over again, including one fierce blow to the skull that had penetrated her brain.

Within minutes, armies of policemen, investigators, Steinberg friends, and Singer family members had invaded the house. Later the police would be accused of incompetence in letting so many people trample the murder scene. Steve Steinberg himself continued to talk distressfully about the "two long-haired men with bushy beards" who had invaded the house through an open patio door and demanded jewelry. Angered at not finding as much as they wanted, one man had held him down while the other killed Elana.

But Steinberg could not look Elana's parents in the eyes as he told his story, and the police could find no sign that strangers had been in the house that night.

Searchers then found, tucked between the box spring of the bed and the bed platform, a bloody carving knife with a ten-inch blade. There had been no "men with bushy beards," only a very disturbed husband and father who had taken a knife from his own kitchen with which to kill his charming, tiny wife. When they found a small collection of valuable jewelry piled neatly behind a mirror in the bathroom—the mirror over the man's vanity table—they took Steven Steinberg from the hospital, where the cut on his palm had been stitched, to the police station not far down the road from beautiful McCormick Ranch.

At 5:30 A.M., as the sun was rising over the land where people hoped their dreams would come true, Steven Steinberg was booked for the murder of his wife.

The Defense

Steinberg went to trial eight months later. But the intricately choreographed and thoroughly buttressed defense turned the case into a trial of Elana Steinberg, the victim.

Steve's attorney, Robert Hirsh, assisted by Mike Benchoff, pleaded Steinberg not guilty by reason of temporary insanity. They had as their prime defense psychiatrist Dr. Martin Blinder of San Francisco, who had testified in the Dan White case and who, earlier, had developed the precedent-setting defense of Albert Berry, which had tried to persuade a jury to acquit him on the basis that his wife was suicidal and had coerced her husband into murdering her.

Dr. Blinder flew from California to meet with Steinberg and came away to write a report that excoriated Elana as a money-grubbing, nagging, shrewish wife who kept her husband firmly under her control, until his mind "snapped." Another psychiatrist, Dr. Donald Holmes, agreed that Steinberg was in an "altered state of consciousness" at the time of the murder and added another useful tidbit: that Steinberg, who had been known to sleepwalk as a child, had been walking in his sleep when he got the knife and killed his wife.

Hirsh found numerous witnesses who happily testified that Steve was a wonderful, friendly person who had the misfortune to have a wife who always wanted more, more, more; that even when he was unemployed and having trouble finding a job, she was hunting for a bigger car, a grander house. They included in the scathing indictment of Elana her mother who, Hirsh said, passed on to Elana the "family trait" of devoting her life "to show for others." They said that admiration was vitally important to the pair, to always have something new and original—and "perfect"—to show their friends . . . or, rather, *her* friends. Elana made the choice of whom they would see (the more illustrious and wealthy, the better), how they would spend their evenings (dining out at expensive restaurants, or giving small, intimate, and costly parties), how the house would be decorated.

In his own book, *Lovers, Killers, Husbands and Wives*, Dr. Blinder told the Steinberg story using pseudonyms. He described the painful procedure he went through getting Steve, in jail, to tear away the veil of his belief that his wife was everything perfect and to begin admitting that, indeed, that was not the case. When the doctor commented that Elana must have been proud of him, Steinberg *hmmm*ed and finally said, "Well, actually, that wasn't [her] way . . ." Apparently she never thanked him for the things he did for her, just expected more the next time. While he faithfully kissed her and said he loved her each night, she never replied, just turned over and went to sleep. When, toward the end, he developed severe headaches each evening, she nagged him about those, too.

The defense claimed that Steinberg's gambling had started just recently, when he turned to it as a way of fulfilling Elana's demands for more money. "When Steve won, it was great," but "nobody liked Steve when he lost. So the gambling became a rather furtive secret activity—when he lost, he told no one." And Elana continued to spend, even as their income dropped drastically when Steve lost his job with the restaurants. Hirsh concluded: "This man was strangled, suffocating in this tension [from trying to keep Elana happy] that has all but enveloped him when he awoke on May 27. He wakes up and Elana has twenty-six stab wounds."

When the coroner testified about those wounds, he described all but four of them with the term "superficial," which to him meant that they did not go into an organ, they went through skin or fat, or into bone. The jury, however, took the word "superficial" to mean that the wounds were little more than mere scratches, the type of rather weak blows that a person sleepwalking might have made. Dr. Holmes reinforced that explanation when he pointed out that there was "a great deal of significance in the wounds pattern." It was "aimless, with a 'stitching' pattern that didn't aim to inflict any fatal wound..."

If Steinberg killed in his sleep, why did he hide the knife and pull out drawers as if someone had been searching the room? Donald Holmes, one of the defense psychiatrists, said that Steve's conscious was denying that the murder had taken place, that when Elana's screams woke him from his sleepwalking, he could not absorb what he had done and so he cleaned up as if the murder had not taken place. That explained why he held on for several days to his story of intruders committing the murder, why it was difficult for him to come to accept that the face of the murderer he saw in his nightmares was his.

Again, if Steinberg killed in his sleep, why didn't the pain of cutting his own hand on the blade wake him? Dr. Holmes testified that there was plenty of evidence in medical literature of sleepwalkers enduring considerable pain, even self-inflicted, and not knowing that they had done it when they awoke. When Steve's hand slipped and he clutched the blade itself to stab with the knife, he was aware of no pain. When he awoke, the blood he found coming from his hand was a complete surprise.

The Steinbergs' friends testified almost en masse in behalf of Steve, perhaps not realizing what the total effect of their stories would be. The jury quickly developed an antipathy toward Elana, viewing her as difficult to satisfy, very status conscious, aggressive, treating Steve as just a source of money, without a serious side to her, thinking only in terms of "black and white," a spendthrift, a "professional shopper," frivolous, shrill, domineering, lacking interest in sex, pushy, and ultimately, a "Jewish American Princess." The latter was a phrase both Steve himself and others used about his wife.

Steve, on the other hand, was shown to be warm, sympathetic, good-humored, gentle, philosophical, charming, reliable, low-key, a hard worker, passive but not a patsy. But the total picture given was of a sucker who tried to do his best for his sharklike wife, but who could never measure up to her expectations.

Steven Steinberg himself took the stand and cried through much of his testimony. Because so much that was bad about Elana and their marriage had been said by others, he was able to continue to be gentle, philosophical, low-key, and charming. He rued the fact that the two of them had not been able to discuss anything, that they just talked "at" each other. He matter-of-factly described the state of his finances at the time of Elana's death—he had to borrow money "from Elana" to get gas for his car.

As the trial ended, the prosecution moved that second-degree murder be given as an option to the first-degree murder charge. That would allow the jury to find Steinberg guilty of an intentional but unpremeditated killing. However, Judge Marilyn Riddel would not allow the change. She felt that the minute or so it took Steinberg to go to the kitchen and get the long knife amounted to premeditation and, therefore, that the second-degree charge would not be valid. The jury, however, took "premeditation" to mean that Steve would have had to think about and plan the murder hours, perhaps days, ahead of time. And it was without the second-degree option among their choices that the jury went into seclusion to decide Steven Steinberg's fate.

Their deliberations did not take long. After a total of only five hours (late one afternoon and early the next morning), the jury arrived at a verdict.

On February 18, 1982, they found Steven Steinberg not guilty by reason of insanity. "There's no justice, no justice at all," said his mother-in-law, who took custody of Traci and Shawn.

Arizona law required that such a verdict be followed immediately by a hearing to determine whether the defendant should be committed to a state mental hospital. Both the prosecution and the defense told the judge that there was no evidence that Steven Steinberg was a danger to either himself or anyone else. The judge agreed, and the man who had killed his "free-spending shrew" of a wife was released.

In the weeks that followed the release of Steven Steinberg, the judge was blamed by the public for letting "a killer go free" by her decision not to allow a second-degree murder verdict. An editorial in the *Scottsdale Daily Progress* said: "There is something wrong with our system of justice when such a brutal crime can be committed and can go unpunished even though the facts of the killing are admitted."

Ultimately, the Arizona legislature changed state law so that instead of the prosecution having to disprove the defense's contention of insanity, the defense must now actively prove the insanity.

It was discovered after the trial that among the jewelry that was supposedly stolen the night of the murder were some earrings that Steve had earlier claimed had been stolen during a trip to Las Vegas. Because his insurance company had paid for them, there was considerable talk of his being indicted for insurance fraud. But it didn't happen.

In 1988, Shirley Frondorf, an Arizona attorney, wrote a book called *Death of a "Jewish American Princess"* in which she demonstrates quite clearly that Steve was a compulsive gambler and had been since his days in Chicago. Even before he and Elana were married, he had come to need the incredible "high" that gambling brings to some people—the same high as drugs or alcohol give to others. The only difference was that after their marriage, he had to try to keep his ever greater losses secret from Elana.

Steve Steinberg, finding himself unwelcome wherever he went, changed his name and moved away from Arizona, seeking a new life elsewhere.

5

The Nightmare of the American Dream
Dan White

> They had it coming, and besides, he couldn't help himself.
>
> Dan Weiss of Dan White's defense,
> in *The San Francisco Killings*

He was called "All-American boy," "idealist," "clean cut," "a physical man," "righteous," "uncompromising," "man of the people." But there was a negative side to those epithets that only a few recognized: "quitter," "inflexible," "unfeeling," "loner," "depressed." On November 10, 1978, the Dan White of that latter list acquired a new epithet: "murderer."

Dan was born into the solidly conservative, Irish-Catholic, working-class society of 1940s San Francisco, the second oldest of nine children. His father, the parent he was closest to, was a fireman, often away for long stretches of time but nurturing when he was at home. His mother did what she needed to, to take care of her large family, but when his father was gone, Dan often felt like the odd man out in his family. He got none of the respect that the oldest child received, and none of the caring that was the natural right of the younger ones.

Dan seemed to have been born wanting to do the right thing. The problem was that others weren't always in agreement about what the "right thing" was. In addition, his own definition of what was right could readily be changed. He had a temper, which sometimes exploded into fights, but he usually used it to defend others—something for which he often did not get credit. After his father died, he felt unable to live up to his ideals of what an older son of a big Irish family should be, and his grades fell. He was forced to transfer out of his private Catholic school and into a new biracial public high school. There, though, he found himself and became captain of the football team, and student manager as well as third-base coach of the baseball team.

In a moment worthy of a movie script, the Wilson High School baseball team was tied with the snobbish St. Ignatius School. The coach signaled to Dan to bunt because he was followed in the lineup by the two best hitters. But Dan, convinced that he knew what was right in the situation, chose to ignore the signal. When the coach angrily told him that there could be only one person calling the signals on a team, Dan tore off his uniform and stormed out of the game and off the team. Later, people with long memories would recall this episode as an early example of quitting when he couldn't get his own way. He saw it as an example of knowing that he was right and not being willing to give in.

White set standards for himself, especially in physical achievement, that were often not possible to live up to. Failing, his self-esteem would take a nosedive, and he would respond by setting even higher standards. The perfectionist in him did not allow room for failure. So if he saw himself failing at something, he quit instead of seeing it through.

Dan White was a compulsive eater, though he probably never knew it, and only the fact that he lived such a physical life (also rather compulsively) up to the time of his election kept him from being fat. He learned early, probably in the rejection he felt from his family, to take comfort in food. It kept the anger suppressed, it mollified the fear, it alleviated the hurts. So when life got to be too much for him and he felt himself heading for an explosion, he binged on sugary foods, turned the potential explosion into a depression, and disappeared from active life while he rode it out.

All this meant that when he became truly angry about something—heading for an explosion—he had no experience in handling it. He had learned in childhood that temper tantrums were not acceptable, but he had not acquired an adequate substitute . . . except pretending that the anger wasn't there, a pretense he could keep up only with the support of sugar, which, in some people, has the same effect as alcohol.

With an inadequate sense of self-esteem, he had a deep

need to be appreciated by others. When the appreciation was not forthcoming, he would abandon what he was doing and look for greener pastures. His first job after serving in Vietnam in the army was as a policeman, a job in which he was sure that he was going to be able to live up to his goal of being something important in the community.

At first it was exciting being an undercover narcotics cop, working with and getting to know the people on the street. But Dan couldn't stand having to arrest those people when the evidence was all in; after all, those people didn't appreciate what he was doing. Nor were things any different when he transferred to street duty. One night he found several officers working over a prisoner and Dan turned them in. No, his fellow policemen didn't appreciate Dan either, because he had broken the unspoken code. Finding himself alone with his righteousness, he quit, took what money he had, and set out to travel the country a bit and even made a side trip to Ireland.

On his return to San Francisco, Dan, certain that everyone appreciated firemen, joined the fire department that had been his idolized father's work. He graduated among the top students in his class at the fire academy and even spoke at graduation, a fact that would soon hold him in good stead. Soon he had two commendations for heroism, recognition that would help him when he tried to move into a new category of public service.

* * *

Public Service, Public Failure

As Dan White was maturing, he discovered that his beloved San Francisco was changing around him, changing into a city he did not recognize and of which he felt no part. As tourism became more important than shipping, and nightlife more important than families, Dan found himself more and more at odds with the way things were going. His idealistic streak told him that perhaps there was something he could do to help preserve the way of life he loved, and the 1977 election of the Board of Supervisors gave him the opportunity to try. It was the first election of supervisors by districts, instead of the previous method of citywide elections, which had long been controlled by representatives of the well-to-do parts of town. Never mind that he didn't know anything about politics. He knew hundreds of blue-collar people in all walks of life in his district, and they all recognized him as one of their own. They wanted to take their city back from the "radicals, social deviates, and incorrigibles," as Dan called the forces he was prepared to fight.

"You have to change how things are done *before* crime takes place," he told Dr. Martin Blinder. "You have to change things from the top. I knew that most of the people out there in the neighborhoods agreed with me. I believed that *I* could do something—I could really make some changes."

Prominent among the people he wanted to fight was George Moscone, the mayor of San Francisco. White knew from his police days that Moscone, a married man, was regularly arrested with whores and then quietly released by police who kept no record of his arrests, in return, probably, for favors.

White put his soul and his savings into the campaign, managing to walk virtually every street in his district, knock on every door, shake every hand. His good-looking personal appeal did what his nonexistent platform could not—got him elected by a large margin.

From day one, Dan was out of his depth on the Board of Supervisors. He had no specific plans that he wanted to implement, no goals toward which he wanted to work. He only knew that he wanted to try to keep things as they had been when he was a child. He initiated no important legislation, just reacted to other people's proposals, either for or against.

Political reality and compromise had no meaning for him. Either he believed something from the depths of his childhood roots or he didn't care. If he cared, compromise was not possible because, for him, compromise was a sign of weakness. "Tit for tat" was not possible. And he regarded those people who compromised on one issue in order to gain support on another as having sold themselves out. He got no pleasure in having power, and did not know what to do with the power he had acquired. He gave the appearance of power, however, in that numerous uniformed policemen and firemen, who regarded Dan as something of a hero, often hung around his office at City Hall.

His major problem was that the city attorney ruled that his job with the fire department was "incompatible" with his position as a supervisor. As a fireman he had been earning over eighteen thousand dollars a year. As a supervisor he would earn less than ten thousand; most supervisors had additional jobs, many of them with direct involvement with the city government. But he and his wife, Mary Ann, decided that they could manage, so he gave up the fire department position.

The strikes were against Dan White: he had given up a job he loved for one that was turning out to be very different from the way he had thought it would be.

In his do-gooder mode, newly elected Supervisor White had gone to Dianne Feinstein, who was president of the Board of Supervisors, and asked her to give Supervisor Harvey Milk a committee chairmanship he coveted, an appointment she had initially rejected. The two men had absolutely nothing in common. Milk was a New York Jew who took pride in becoming the first overtly out-of-the-closet homosexual to be elected to major office; he called himself the "Number One Queen." Every liberal cause Milk favored was anathema to Dan White, who did not understand Milk's humor, sexuality (which he regarded as perversion), willingness to be an underdog, or vision of San Francisco's future.

Because of his action in going to see Feinstein on Harvey's behalf, White expected Harvey Milk to vote with him against turning a Portola Heights convent that had a tradition of taking care of wayward girls into an officially supported home for juveniles, called the Youth Campus. Milk, pressured by White, said that he was certainly inclined to do so, a comment that Dan took as a promise, especially when Dan's committee, urged by

Harvey Milk, voted to recommended that San Francisco enact gay rights legislation, the first in the nation.

Dan felt justified in inviting his supporters to the Board meeting when the Youth Campus came up for a vote. The people who had put him into office would have a chance to see just how good he was at living up to his campaign promise to keep the juvenile delinquents out of their neighborhood. But there, in public, Harvey Milk voted in favor of the Youth Campus and made the passing vote. Humiliated, unable to pass the vote off as an example of politics in action, Dan stormed out of the Board chambers and stayed away from City Hall for several days, sulking, depressed, and eating. When he returned, he paid Milk back by voting against the gay rights ordinance—the only supervisor to do so. But still he thought of himself as the homosexual supervisor's friend.

The sacrifice of his job as a fireman also began to pinch, and he knew he would have to find another source of income. Ray Sloan, his aide, found a political sympathizer in the developer of Pier 39, a waterfront tourist arcade, who offered Dan a fast-food business in a prime spot in the arcade. By taking a second mortgage on their house, he and a pregnant Mary Ann were able to buy the lease on a fast-food place called the Hot Potato. He did not see it as "selling out" when he used his political support to get Pier 39 past the city's Art Commission, which tried to stop the work until they had approved the plans. But those supervisors who had been castigated by

White for "selling their vote" on other matters just chuckled knowingly.

Although Dan had been voted into his position with an overwhelming majority and every show of support from his constituents, during the early summer there was an attempt to recall him. In addition, a charge was made that he had taken some illegal campaign contributions. The latter was disproved by the district attorney and the former failed, but the two attempts by his detractors left the wonder boy angry and bitter.

Countdown to Death

In June 1978, Californians passed the famous Proposition 13, which would henceforth limit property taxes. George Moscone responded by proposing a bill that would put new taxes on the downtown businesses of San Francisco to offset the property tax losses. Any new taxes. had to be in the works by July 1, before Proposition 13 went into effect and banned new local taxes. Moscone was able to persuade Dan that his city needed his help and that he should vote for the new taxes. Dan voted in favor at the preliminary vote, but when the meeting turned into an acrimonious discussion on trying to tax the Giants' receipts at Candlestick Park because one supervisor was angry at the seat given him at baseball games, Dan left, despairing at his lack of ability to achieve what he wanted in the pettiness of City Hall.

He was vulnerable when a group from the Chamber of Commerce arranged a "Friends of Dan White" party that would repay the money his campaign owed him personally. The casual talk of the rich men whom Dan admired persuaded him that it would not be a good thing to vote in favor of taxes on the downtown businesses. He didn't, and Dan White now had an angry Mayor Moscone against him. Then, the next month, Dan also failed to support Moscone on an attempt to settle a minority discrimination suit against the police.

Dan, tired from the combination of his supervisor's position, working late into the night at the Hot Potato, taking care of his tiny baby when Mary Ann was working, and getting no exercise, was becoming more and more withdrawn. Feeling a failure because his upbringing did not allow a man to have a working wife, he became irritable with anyone who challenged him in any way. Now he trusted only the people he had known for many years, and those only if they were firemen or policemen. He began to neglect his office, staying home for long days at a time, isolating himself and eating doughnuts and potato chips and soft drinks, unable to move beyond the morass of self-pity that he had constructed for himself.

He was convinced that a "true man" would never stop fighting for what he believed in, but he just didn't seem to know how to fight anymore. The City Hall world did not function in any way that he understood. The last straw came when the Board was voting to approve closing some narrow hillside streets for a bicycle race. Dan felt that it was a dangerous route because in an emergency vehicles would be unable to get through. He asked the sponsoring supervisor to have the route changed by his constituents, but the supervisor said that just wasn't possible: "These people own me."

Dan White, appalled at the cynicism, writhed at what he saw as the corruption of City Hall.

On the morning of November 10, the self-pity still clinging to him, he chose the method that he had used before—with the baseball team when he was in high school, and with the police force when his idealistic need to help others was trounced on by the reality of working within a system he failed to understand. He decided to quit. That was the most positive action he could think of.

For the first time in days, he shaved and dressed nicely. Presenting himself to Mary Ann at the Hot Potato, he told her what he wanted to do. She, loath ever to disagree with him, saw how relieved he looked and just said quietly, as she usually did, "If you think that's best." His secretary typed the letter of resignation to Moscone, in which Dan said the resignation was ". . . due to personal responsibilities which I feel must take precedence over my legislative duties . . ."

Moscone, reading the letter, asked Dan to come see him. The mayor did not plead with Dan to change his mind. He just listened quietly to his story of being unable to take care of his family properly and then said, "You do what you have to do." Nothing was said about corruption, the inability to come to terms with reality, the lack of substantive legislation proposed by Dan.

Dan's first reaction was an immense feeling of relief. During the next day or so he was able to breathe deeply and enjoy playing with his family for the first time in weeks. Harvey Milk's reaction consisted of great glee because he knew that Dan was planning to vote against his pet project, a gay community center. Milk hurried to Moscone and demanded that he make an interim appointment of someone who would vote for the center. Moscone agreed.

On the following Monday, White's resignation letter was officially read into the record and the Board voted to accept it. However, phone calls were coming in from all over, expressing anger at Dan's quitting. Tuesday morning, Ray Sloan and Dan's secretary, disturbed at the reactions, decided to try to get Dan to ask for his resignation back. They thought it was possible because Moscone needed the support of Dan's district when he ran for reelection. After they talked to Dan's mother and learned that the family had gathered a large sum of money as a noninterest loan to Dan that might help relieve his financial burden, they went to see the glumly sulking Dan, hoping that he would feel challenged to come back. He quickly acknowledged that the real problem was not his family but City Hall.

"I'm not a crybaby but those people down there are basic shits. I just chose not to be part of it," he said.

When he acknowledged that he was different from the others at City Hall, Ray brought up his challenge: "You're afraid [Moscone] won't give you your seat back, is that it?" Certain that, in fact, Moscone would not, Dan tried to show Ray that he was not a quitter. He called the mayor and told him that he wanted his letter of resignation back. Moscone agreed to give it to him. Dan picked up the letter that evening, certain that he was once again a supervisor. He was wrong, because legal advisers to the mayor convinced Moscone that they had to look into the legalities of rescinding the resignation, because the Board had already acted on it, making it official.

When Dan saw Moscone the next day, George pointed out the problem but promptly added that he would definitely reappoint Dan to the position, as it was the mayor's privilege to do. He confirmed that promise with reporters. But to the furious Harvey Milk, who still expected Moscone to deliver on his promise to appoint someone who would vote for the gay community center, Moscone said not to worry about it.

During the next several days, Moscone began to see that he had himself in a bind. He had promised the appointment to Dan, but he was being reminded right, left, and center that others would hold it against him at reelection time if he made Dan a supervisor again. Goldie Judge, who had been one of Dan's original supporters but later turned against him, quickly put together a rally of people who thought that Dan had deserted them and disgraced their district and should not be reappointed. Another former supporter told reporters that he thought that Dan White held the people in his district "in utter contempt," while Goldie shouted at Dan to "go peel potatoes!" When this event was discussed on television that night, Moscone realized that Dan White could not, in fact, deliver his district to him at election time. The mayor no longer had any reason to deliver on his promise to reappoint Dan to the supervisor's seat.

The downtown business people and realtors whom Dan had helped with his vote against more business taxes quickly put together a rally in support of Dan, but it did nothing to change Moscone's mind. On Saturday, November 18, Moscone asked Dan to come see him at City Hall. The mayor, still apparently sympathetic (because he could not bear to hurt people in person), explained that Dan just did not have the support behind him that he needed for Moscone to appoint him . . . unless he could come up with proof of support in the form of petitions and letters, and unless Moscone could feel sure that Dan would be with him when critical votes came up. Dan ignored the latter requirement and promised Moscone that he would demonstrate that he had the support of his constituents.

Dan and his secretary spent the weekend mailing out requests for letters urging his reappointment. It was the same weekend that the world learned of the horror of over nine hundred deaths at Jim Jones's People's Temple in Guyana. The Temple had previously been in San Francisco, where Jones had been Moscone's housing commissioner.

On Monday, November 20, Moscone realized that Dan thought that he had made a definite commitment to reappoint him if he could get a show of support. He released to the press a letter to Dan in which he said, "I must reiterate that I have not made a commitment of any kind to appoint you. . . ." Even then Dan was unwilling to realize that the game was over, that he was inextricably caught up in Moscone's inability to be upfront with the truth. Once again he zoomed down the emotional slide into depression. The only plan he had was to attend a supervisors' meeting on the following Monday and forcibly take his seat.

The next day, the *San Francisco Chronicle* printed a snide item about White's supposedly unsolicited letters of support coming in as identical photocopies. Although Dan was not willing to make any further effort to save himself, his aides devised a plan to go to court and obtain a temporary restraining order preventing Moscone from appointing anyone else to the seat, a plan that Dan White did not agree with. By Wednesday, the day before Thanksgiving, as legal opinions were flying, rumors spread that several Jim Jones adherents were on their way to San Francisco to carry out some assassinations. A metal detector was installed at the main City Hall entrance.

On the national holiday, Dan White, certain that he was worthless and loathsome, restlessly prowled his study at home, brooding over resentments of the past, sulking about his present feeling of helplessness, and unable to envision a future. The next day, Mary Ann left to attend a friend's wedding in Omaha, Nebraska, leaving Dan to take care of baby Charlie while she was gone. He spent the entire long weekend eating only what munchy, sugary food came readily to hand, while at City Hall, the forces were lining up to prevent any recognition of Dan White if he should actually try to take his seat on Monday. The temporary restraining order was refused.

On Sunday evening, Mary Ann returned to San Francisco.

She tried to tell the distracted Dan about her weekend, but his attention was not available. Also by that evening, plans were laid by Moscone to announce the appointment of Don Horanzy to the vacant supervisor's position. Everyone, including the press, knew that it was going to happen the next morning. But no one had the courage to tell Dan White that his cause was lost.

After Mary Ann went to bed, Dan left the house to wander downtown, stopping at a bookstore and purchasing a copy of Jill and Leon Uris's book, *Ireland: A Terrible Beauty*. As he was preparing for bed, a CBS News reporter, Barbara Taylor, called and said that she had heard that he was definitely not getting the appointment the next day, though she did not know who would. Holding in his anger at getting the news in such a way, Dan simply said, "I don't have anything to say."

Convinced that he had let everybody in his life down, Dan returned to brooding and pacing. He read his new book for a while, perhaps marveling at the idea, described in the book, that an act performed in rage could have redeeming power.

Monday, November 27. Dan White had not slept, and his self-loathing only increased when Mary Ann had to rush off to the Hot Potato to slice potatoes. Such promises he had made to his wife—he had not been able to keep them. Such promises others had made to him—they had not kept them either. If they had, perhaps he could have kept his commitments to his wife.

When his secretary called, all she could report, in tears, was that George Moscone had deliberately maneuvered things to avoid accepting the petitions she had so laboriously gathered from Dan's followers. She later reported that she had seen Harvey Milk coming from Moscone's private office. And Dan put Milk and Moscone together as the two who were deliberately trying to hurt him.

Explosion

Suddenly Dan White's helplessness and self-pity were over. He shaved and dressed in his most "I am serious" clothes, then called Denise, his secretary, to come and get him, saying that he was going to "give George and Harvey a piece of his mind."

Dan grabbed his police .38, loaded its five chambers, and placed it in a holster at the back of his belt. As he was leaving the house, he impulsively tore the cover off the Uris book and thrust it in his pocket. He said to Denise as she drove, "I'm a man and I can take it. I just want George to tell me face to face. I want to see his face. I want to go tell Harvey, I went out on a limb for him and why is he doing this to me."

When he reached City Hall, he started to climb the stairs but remembered that the metal detector was there and reversed his direction. The prosecutor later made a big point of that action, insisting that he was already planning to use the gun and did not want to be caught with it. Dan, however, just as firmly insisted that the man on duty at the detector was a stranger and that he did not want to embarrass him. He went around to the side of the building. He no longer had a key to the door at the bottom of the ramp, but he climbed through an open window next to it.

A pale, tired Dan White startled George Moscone's personal assistant by appearing suddenly at her desk. The mayor reluctantly agreed to see White for a minute. When the ex-supervisor bluntly asked Moscone if he was going to be reappointed to the position, the mayor replied no, and said something about White's district not wanting him. White exploded and ranted for a moment about all the support he had from the voters, but Moscone cut him short with: "It's just a political decision, Dan. . . . There's nothing more I can say."

It was political decisions that had defied Dan White's understanding all these months, and here was another sealing his death warrant. That was a mistake. And it was another mistake for Moscone to put his arm around tearful Dan's shoulder and invite him into his private back office for a calming drink. The depressed Dan could not bear to be touched, not even by his wife, with whom he had had no intimate relations in months.

When the apparently sympathetic mayor asked about Dan's plans and added, "Maybe we can help out," something exploded in Dan's head. He pulled out his .38 and fired into Moscone's chest. As the already dying mayor fell forward, the fire took hold of Dan's brain and he fired again and again. Finally, with Moscone on the floor, Dan crouched over him, held his gun close to the mayor's ear, and fired one last bullet.

He stepped out the back door of the office, then ran to the far side of the building toward the back door of the supervisors' communal office, reloading as he ran. The startled Dianne Feinstein did not know that anything was wrong as she said hello. Supervisor Harvey Milk was not delighted to see his nemesis Dan White look into his office, but he emerged willingly when Dan asked to see him for a minute. They went into Dan's old office, now empty, and Dan shut the door.

The anger rolled out of the man who could never show when he was angry. Harvey Milk, like Moscone, made a mistake. He showed his nervousness by making a habitual smirk, one that Dan read as malevolent satisfaction at Dan's predicament. It was the last facial gesture that the "Number One Queen" would make. Dan pulled his gun, fired four times, and finished with another close-to-the-head shot.

Before the other supervisors could do anything but scream, Dan White ran out of the office and down the stairs. He got Denise's car keys from her and quickly drove away. He stopped once at a pay phone and called Mary Ann, asking only that she leave the Hot Potato and meet him at St. Mary's Cathedral. There he knelt in prayer, asking his God's forgiveness, until Mary Ann arrived.

He told her in straightforward statements what he had done and that he was going to give himself up. Once she understood the full horror of the situation, all the good Catholic girl could do was ask that he not commit suicide. Less than an hour after George Moscone and Harvey Milk had died, their killer walked into the police station where he had worked some years before and gave himself up.

"I got kind of fuzzy."

"My head didn't feel right."

"He was talking, an' nothing was gettin' through to me. It was just like a roaring in my ears."

"Then, that was it. Then I, I just shot him. That was it. It was over."

Within minutes after entering the police station, Dan White was confessing into a tape recorder, answering questions put to him by his friend since grade school, Frank Falzon. The policeman listened as Dan, in tears, finished, "I've always been honest and worked hard, never cheated anybody, or, you know, I'm not a crook or anything an' I wanted to do a good job, I'm trying to do a good job an' I saw this city as it's goin' kinda downhill and I was always just a lonely vote on the Board and tryin' to be honest an', an' I just couldn't take it anymore and that's it."

Five months after the murders, Dan White went to trial in the court of Walter F. Calcagno, in San Francisco. There was no doubt about his guilt. The trial was to determine the punishment. The prosecution held that the murders were committed with full deliberation and malice, making them first-degree murders. The defense held that Dan had not left home that morning with the intention of killing Moscone and Milk; that because of the depression he was in, augmented by the junk food he had been consuming in large quantities, his capacity to know right from wrong, and his ability even to form an intention—to premeditate—were diminished; that, therefore, at most, he was guilty of voluntary manslaughter.

Day by day, the lawyers laid out before the jury the pressures that had been mounting on the man, and the kind of man he was. The defense called him a "moral man undone by mental illness and overcome by a heat of passion." They said that his illness would have prevented him from forming the intention to murder.

Psychiatrist Martin Blinder testified, "If it were not for...all the tremendous pressures on him the weeks prior to the shooting, and perhaps if it were not for the ingestion of this aggravating factor, this junk food...I would suspect that these homicides would not have taken place," that the pressures on him would not have had "a profound effect upon him and indeed move him to an unaccustomed state of passion."

Another psychiatrist, Dr. George Solmon, pointed out that Dan White had "a conflict of identity...he was never able to integrate into a meaningful, coherent whole person." Solmon noted that Dan felt inferior to his father, whom he regarded as a hero, "and it was particularly harder to please somebody who is dead than someone who is alive...." But his own negative opinion of himself never allowed him to think that he might have found approval in his father's eyes. Solmon also added, "To me it seems quite inconceivable that Mr. White, who really couldn't even tell off somebody who stepped on his toes in a line, so to speak, would be able to plan, even briefly, something heinous..." such as a murder.

The jury found Dan White guilty of the voluntary manslaughter of Mayor George Moscone and Supervisor Harvey Milk. He would be out of prison in less than five years.

When the large gay population of San Francisco heard the decision, many of them felt that the law was saying, in effect, that it was all right to kill homosexuals. Thousands of them poured into downtown San Francisco and rioted around City Hall. In what came to be called the "White Night Riots," they burned police cars, injured whatever policemen came into their hands, and called for the death of Dan White. One supervisor, Harry Britt, told a reporter, "Society is going to have to deal with us not as nice little fairies who have hairdressing salons, but as people capable of this violence."

After the wreckage was cleared away, a spray-painted sign was found on a wall: HE GOT AWAY WITH MURDER!

In early 1984, five years after his conviction, Dan White was paroled from prison. In the depths of depression, he came home to his wife, who had borne another child by him while he was in prison (as a result of a conjugal visit); the child was born with Down's syndrome.

Again San Francisco swelled in outrage, this time at his release, and rumors flew that a gay would kill him. Threats came at Dan from every direction. He was unable to get a job, and his wife had to support the family. Finally, futility and depression overwhelmed him. Late in 1985, Mr. All-American closed his garage doors, fastened a garden hose to the car's exhaust, started the engine, and died.

PART III

ABANDONMENT
The Unwanted Child

Rejection of a child—abandonment—is one of the critical factors that psychiatrists have found at the core of murder and other crime. A child who perceives himself as abandoned by his parents perceives himself as unloved and, consequently, as unlovable. Most people with such a start in life grow into normal, law-abiding adults, perhaps with enough difficulties getting along in the world to require some therapy, but, like most of us, just surviving and doing the best they can.

For other people, however—again it's the unanswerable "why"—the feeling, or knowledge, that they have been abandoned—put out for adoption, ignored, rejected—becomes the prime factor of their existence, even if the rejection never actually existed in the minds of the parents. These people are convinced that at heart they are nothing, and everywhere they turn, they see evidence of further rejection. Fearing it, such people seek ways to convince themselves that they are not afraid, that they are powerful, that they are in control. They may turn to crime and, if they ever reach the point where they feel themselves being put down beyond the point of tolerance, they may turn to murder.

Yochelson's study of criminal attitudes showed him that criminals fear most "being put down by people or by events. The fear of a put-down is global in the criminal, because a put-down can reduce him to a zero." So he sees put-downs everywhere he goes. It's a put-down, for example, for such a person to have to ask for a ride, so he steals a car. "For a criminal, a put-down occurs when someone else fails to meet his every desire, bend to his will, fulfill his every expectation."

The ultimate abandonment is being put out for adoption. Again, most people survive and find acceptance in their new loving families, but some few do not. David Berkowitz, the Son of Sam, did not learn until he was seven that he was adopted. As an adult he began to search for his real mother. He both found her and began to give in to his demons at the same time. His story is included in Part IV. Kenneth Bianchi, one of the Hillside Stranglers in Los Angeles, was also an adopted child who was never held by loving arms until he was several months old. He learned to use his charm to become one of the "charismatic serial killers" described at the end of the book.

As with a physical injury to the brain, however, the effect of adoption on an individual depends more on the way it is handled within the family than it does on the fact of adoption itself. There is nothing in adoption per se that determines that a child will become antisocial.

In the following tales of murder, the men who perceived themselves as having been abandoned by the world had not experienced that ultimate abandonment of adoption. They experienced rejection in the midst of whatever family life their parents were capable of giving them. That family life was not enough. They got back at the world by killing others in large numbers.

Charlie Starkweather, who felt from earliest childhood that he was continually being put down, reached his limit of toleration when, at eighteen, he was thrown out by his family. When it appeared that his girlfriend, Caril Ann Fugate, was also going to be forced to reject him, he slew her parents, beginning a spree that would destroy the lives of eleven people.

Jack Graham's mother, finding it difficult for a divorced woman to make ends meet, placed him in an orphanage. He probably could have survived that, but he never could accept the reality that when his mother did remarry, she would not let him come home. When his limit of tolerance was reached as an adult, he blew up the airplane she was on, not even caring that forty-three other people would die, too.

Charles Manson must have been aware from infancy that he was unwanted. He never knew from one day to the next who, if anyone, would be taking care of him. Since the whole of his life was one big put-down, he started early to find power in crime. At age twelve, he found himself being turned over to institutions. They didn't do much better, and soon the boys' homes turned into reform schools and then into prisons. As he said many years later, "Policemen raised me, convicts raised me. Administrators raised me." And none of them did a good enough job to prevent him from demonstrating that he wasn't a zero by directing the gory killing of at least nine, possibly as many as thirty, people.

6

The Boy Who
Welcomed Death
Charles Starkweather

> Sometimes the hate was so real I could feel it
> coming to life like something kind of dead or
> asleep and beginning to wake up and stir around.
> Charles Starkweather

He was short, bow-legged, red-haired, myopic, and he
stammered as a child. Feeling inadequate, he was convinced that the world hated him. The only person who
uncritically adored the young man who tried to pretend
he was James Dean was tiny but sexy Caril Ann Fugate,
five years younger than him. When he was threatened
with her loss, he took her along on an eight-day spree in
which eleven people lost their lives.

In the long tales that Charlie Starkweather told the
psychiatrists and reporters who interviewed him after he
was arrested for murdering eleven people and was wait-

ing for death officially to claim him, the nineteen-year-old returned again and again to his first days at school. Although he had never felt loved by his father, whatever security he had known was in his own home. He had left the security of his own backyard to attend kindergarten and, from the first moments, felt as if he were singled out for derision, the same kind that he had always received at home.

Conscious of what he regarded as bowed legs, the anathema of bright red hair, and stammering speech, he decided that the other children were laughing at him. Within his very first free-play period, he found himself being isolated and left out. In organized play, he was the one left standing when the teams had been chosen, and the teacher made him a substitute.

It does not matter that his teachers remember none of that. What matters is that Charlie *believed* those things happened, and thus he started to create a fantasy life in which the feeling that he had been abandoned justified the hatred he felt for those around him. As he grew, he failed to learn ways to compensate for attitudes or inabilities that he thought people held against him. Thus began a career of hate, a brief lifetime of feeling deprived and left out of the good things, an acceptance that only in death would he be equal to others and come into his own. And all of those feelings he blamed on others. *They* were the ones who must pay.

At school, "Little Red" quickly discovered the pleasures of taking out his anger by fighting. He had an easily aroused temper and would willingly throw his husky little body at foes bigger than himself. In writing his own story while he waited for death to come, he said (in his own unedited spelling and grammar): "I fought fast and a little furiously like a mamiac in rage and fury and as I fought sense of outrage grew to striving, to throw, to bend, to hurt and most of all to beat those who teased me . . .

"My fighting repretation stayed with me throughout my school years and even after I had stopped going to school that repetation stayed with me, but my rebellion started against the world and the human race when I was being maded fun at and that being made fun at is what cause my fights when I was a youngster. . . ."

Unfortunately for Charlie, his behavior in class itself was usually adequate. He did not interfere with class enough to be sent to a school psychologist. Perhaps he should have misbehaved more.

While in prison, Charlie was given IQ tests by both the defense and the prosecution. Though the numbers differed a bit (those of the prosecution were higher than those of the defense), they both showed that Charlie was at least average in intelligence, and perhaps even slightly above in some areas. But Charlie had the misfortune to have poor eyesight even as a little child, when most of schooling involves looking at the blackboard. His problem was not diagnosed until he was fifteen, by which time learning had long since passed him by.

The third of eight children, Charlie spent his entire short life in Lincoln, Nebraska. His father was a carpenter and repairman who suffered from ill health, though he taught Charlie and the other boys to hunt and fish. For some reason that never revealed itself, Charlie feared his father and, according to one trial psychiatrist, "took out on other people some of his feelings he may have had toward his own family." His mother raised the family and worked as a waitress after Charlie started school.

Throughout the nine years that Charlie stayed in school, his problems continued to isolate him from his peers. He never reached more than five feet two inches in height, and, while other children reveled in learning new things, he was laughed at for the mistakes he made because of his poor sight. The only incidents that gave him any self-esteem were the fights he won. He came to believe that it was only his hatred that kept him going. Whenever the world got to be too much for him, he would sink into a depression and come out fighting.

He was held back to repeat the sixth grade for reasons of "maturity," but it did no good. At the end of ninth grade, when he was sixteen years old, Charlie Starkweather quit school. He had never found any subject that caught his attention for any length of time or that he felt offered a future. He liked art (and spent considerable time drawing while in prison) but had never learned that he had to work at something to succeed. Apparently he was not able to envision himself in a future and so was not willing to prepare for one. Only his rebellion against a world he was certain he couldn't share stayed with him . . . and grew.

Since childhood, Charlie's favorite activities involved the use of guns and being in the outdoors. He enjoyed hunting, and took pride in always hitting his living targets in the head, though he felt sorry for the little animals he killed. And he became an expert quick draw with a pistol, though he admitted that it was not a terribly useful talent for anyone except a lawman. He wrote: "It is true that I have always been an out door sportsman, firearms besides automobiles, and besides that of my family, have been my ruling passion, but between the firearms, and automobiles, I rather hear the crack of a firearm than have, or drive the finist car in the whole wide world."

His fascination with guns expanded into a fascination with the whole subject of killing and death. He came to believe that in death everyone was equal and that therefore death would not be such a bad thing. Then Charlie Starkweather would be just like everyone else. He began to see death as a goal, a place to be where he did not have to keep up the burden of hate that threatened to bury him.

After leaving school, Charlie went to work full-time at a newspaper warehouse. Not long after he started, the handle of a paper-baling machine slipped as he was working and struck him on the left side of his head, knocking him out and cutting the corner of his eye. The cut healed with a few stitches, but afterward he had almost perpetual headaches for the few years remaining to him. It is likely that Charlie's head injury and the emotional drag of continual pain played some role in his killings, much as in the cases of Richard Speck and Charles Whitman, whom we will meet in Part V.

Oddly enough, the fighting was what, in part, let Charlie back into the fellowship of others: most of his friends came from the circle of boys he had fought and bested. He never held his success over them; instead, he was known as friendly and generous. His best friend was Bob Von Busch, whom he fought until they both agreed to fight no more, when they met in the ninth grade. It was Bob who, at seventeen, introduced Charlie to Caril Ann Fugate. She was the younger sister of the girl Bob was dating. She had just turned thirteen.

Caril Ann

It is impossible to talk about Charlie without also talking about Caril Ann. She was with him on the eight-day murder spree that sent him to the electric chair. But their stories differed on her involvement. She claimed that she had been a hostage the entire time, believing that if she tried to get away, Starkweather would kill her family. And yet, one of the first things she said to the deputy sheriff was that her own family—her mother, stepfather, and two-and-a-half-year-old half-sister—had already been murdered by "Chuck" when she arrived home from school. Ultimately, Caril was sentenced to life in prison for her participation in one murder.

When the pair met, Caril changed Charlie's life profoundly. He found her quite grown up (meaning that she wore makeup, swore a lot, and was willing to sleep with him), and since she appeared to like him uncritically, he was drawn to her. The work he did as a garbageman gave him no feeling of a future or participation in adult life, but being with Caril did. "I don't know why it was," he later wrote, "but being alone with her was like owning a little world all our own. . . ."

Caril Ann liked his bowed legs, found his short stature just right for her, and "loved every hair" on his head. He saw that if she liked him, he must be better than he had ever seen himself to be. His speech impediment had disappeared as he grew, but "I forgot about my bow-legs when me and Caril was having excitement." In his death cell he wrote, "I used to want to shoot up the world for no reason, I used to want to throw garbage in some-body's face, I was mad at the world. Then Caril made things clear; then everythin' had a reason. I knowed the end was comin', but it had a reason too."

After Caril had an accident driving his car and Charlie got a ticket for letting an unlicensed driver use his car, two important changes took place in Charlie's life. First, he quit his full-time job so that he would be free in the afternoons to pick Caril up at school and drive her home. He returned to the garbage-collection truck that he had worked at part-time before quitting school. And second, Charlie's father, Guy Starkweather, who had borrowed money to help pay for Charlie's car, tried to make his son promise not to let Caril drive it again. When Charlie refused to do so, the two had a serious fight in which Guy drove Charlie through a window, then told him to get out of the house and stay out. Charlie's view of himself, as less important than an old car, was confirmed.

Charlie moved into a rooming house where he could stay when he paid his rent and where he found the door locked against him when he didn't. At those times, increasingly frequent as time went on, he lived in his car.

Usually Charlie's inability to pay his rent came from spending too much money on Caril. That activity was the joy of his life, even putting the care of his hot rod second. He even opened a joint savings account with her so that she would have access to his money. He would buy her gold jewelry, but shop for his own clothes in a second-hand store. All the attention to detail he gave his own appearance focused on making his hair as much as possible like the late movie actor James Dean's. Like many other youths of the 1950s, he could turn his pompadour into a thing of artistry, even though he begrudged its persistent redness.

When Starkweather was forced to sleep in his car, he often parked at the Crest service station on Lincoln's Cornhusker Highway and spent much of the night chatting with the night manager, Bob McClung, who would wake him at 4:30 to go to work on his garbage route. After McClung was replaced by another man, it was at this service station that Charlie first tested out his ability to kill.

James Reinhardt wrote in *The Murderous Trail of Charles Starkweather:* "Such a killer does not start shooting down real people immediately. There is a time of fantasy building, a time in which the imagination plays upon murder scenes, when the quick draw is simulated, when the firing piece is nursed, and studied, and handled with almost childlike affection. The potential murderer of this type probably does not believe in the beginning stages of fantasy play that he will someday be a real killer... [but] the time came when the *ego* demands could no longer be contained in the inner-world of his fantasy."

That time came when Chuck and Caril started talking about going away together, away from all the hate that separated them from others and gave them "a little world all their own."

For that they needed money.

The First Death

The always-broke Charles Starkweather's first murder occurred for the superficial reasons that are easiest for the rest of us to comprehend: he killed during the course of a robbery in order to prevent the victim from identifying him. However, it was not an unplanned event. From the moment that he decided to rob the service station, he knew that he would have to shoot the new manager, Robert Colvert, if Colvert recognized him. As if to make sure that would happen, Starkweather went into the station twice the night of November 30–December 1, 1957, and chatted with Colvert. Then, after 3:00 A.M., he donned a mask, covered his hair, and went in again, shotgun pointed.

Charlie took his time with the deed, making Colvert turn out lights, hiding in a doorway in case someone drove by, trying to get Colvert to open the safe. He made the attendant get into the car and drive out to a deserted road. There Colvert tried to grab the gun, they fought, and—according to Starkweather, who later claimed to have never killed except in self-defense—it went off in the struggle. When Colvert tried to get up again, Charlie shot him through the head.

Charlie slept several hours and then proudly went to tell Caril that he had pulled off a robbery, but he said that someone else had killed Colvert. He was certain, however, that Caril knew he had done it. He was feeling powerful and at ease with the world he hated, overjoyed at having discovered that killing a human being did not bother him—a fact that made him feel enjoyably superior to the common run of man. He had been willing to die but instead had killed.

"I learned somethin', somethin' that I already knowed, that a man could have money without haulin' garbage." His headaches eased, and he slept well at night, especially after paying his rent and returning to his room.

Caril and Charlie had a good time with the money he got from the robbery—little more than a hundred dollars. They went to movies (all gun-filled action), ate the kinds of junk food that Caril's family did not allow her to have at home, bought comic books . . . and talked of all the things they could do if they got even more money. Having obtained money in an "easy" way, Charlie lost interest in making it on the garbage route and he was soon fired. That gave him more time to work on changing his car from light blue to black.

Bit by bit, as the money ran out, Charlie's hatred and feeling of inferiority surfaced again, his headaches returned, and he was certain that something else important was about to happen. But he didn't know that it would start with

Caril's parents trying once again to break him and Caril up, though she would later claim that she had broken up with him herself.

"If We'd Been Let Alone We Wouldn't Hurt Nobody"

Tuesday, January 21, 1958. Charles Starkweather had been locked out of his rented room again and was forced to sleep in freezing weather in the garage where he kept the hot rod he worked on. He developed a cold that made him feel lousy, and Caril's mother and stepfather, convinced that he would never amount to anything, were demanding that the pair split up. Chuck went to the home of his brother, Rodney, and borrowed a .22, ostensibly to go hunting with Caril's stepfather, Marion Bartlett. (Her own father, William Fugate, was an alcoholic sexual deviate whom she rarely saw.)

From that point on, exactly what happened depends on which story one believes—Caril's, one of Starkweather's, or another. The major point of difference is whether Caril was present or not. She claimed that her parents were not in the house when she got home from school, Chuck having already killed them and tucked their bodies out of sight. He claimed the same thing at first, but later stopped protecting her. He then said that he picked Caril up at school and they arrived at her house together, where they confronted her angry parents. Since there was no trial on the Bartlett murders and no evidence was introduced, we can never know for sure. The following story, however, is based primarily on Starkweather's most detailed confession—Starkweather, a young man who was known around Lincoln for the variety of the lies he told.

The "runty bantam" arrived at the Bartlett home in the early afternoon and gave Velda Bartlett two large rug samples he had found in the trash. She ignored Charlie, focusing her attention on a crying two-and-a-half-year-old, Betty Jean. Marion never appeared. When Charlie, tired of waiting, finally asked if they were going hunting, Velda told him to leave and not come back, and to leave Caril alone. Their argument heated up, until finally Velda struck Charlie in the face. He stormed out and drove around, then returned to get his brother's gun. This time Marion was present, and he physically kicked Charlie out, with a boot to the rear end.

And so rage made the decision.

Charlie went to a pay phone in the nearby grocery store and called Marion Bartlett's employers to tell them that Bartlett would not be at his job as a night watchman for several nights because he was ill. Returning to the Bartletts' house, he waited on the back porch for Caril to come home; he had discovered that his car wasn't working right, and he could not drive to pick her up.

After Caril's return, he heard her and her mother quarreling. Hurrying in, he confronted Velda, who accused him of making Caril pregnant (she wasn't) and began to hit him in the head again. When Charlie returned a blow, Marion joined in the fight and tried to carry Charlie out of the house. Charlie got away, grabbed the .22 from the bedroom, and fired it when Marion started to come after him with a claw hammer. Charlie Starkweather, the boy who bragged that he always hit his prey in the head, did the same to his girlfriend's father.

When Velda Bartlett charged Charlie with a long butcher knife in her hand, Caril may have grabbed the gun and threatened to shoot her mother, but Charlie took it away and pulled the trigger. With a bullet in the side of her head, Velda headed for her baby daughter. Instead of picking her up, however, she turned on Charlie again, who hit her twice with the butt of the rifle. He then turned and gave another blow to little Betty Jean, who was screaming. When that didn't stop her, he grabbed the butcher knife and threw it. The long blade struck the child in the throat, silencing her. Returning to the living room, Charlie found Marion Bartlett still moving, so he used his hunting knife on him.

Sudden silence reigned in the house of death.

Charlie turned on the TV because the silence bothered him. Incredibly, Caril quickly became absorbed in the afternoon programs, while Charlie cleaned up. He wrapped Velda Bartlett's body in a quilt and rug, tying the bundle with clothesline. He dragged it to the old outhouse behind the residence and stuffed it down the toilet hole. He put the little girl's body, still bleeding, into a grocery box and took it, too, out to the outhouse. Charlie wrapped Marion Bartlett's body in a sheet, an army blanket, and finally building paper. He had to remove the screen door to get the body outside, where he placed it inside a chicken coop and placed a screen door over it. He cleaned up the blood, and then walked to the grocery store to stock up on the pair's favorite snacks—Pepsi Cola and potato chips.

Charlie Starkweather and Caril Ann Fugate lived in the murder house for six days, eating snacks, watching TV, and having sex, which seemed particularly intense and enjoyable to Charlie. It must have seemed a fantasy time for Charlie—just the two of them in a "place of their own," with no one putting pressure on them to do anything but enjoy themselves. Charlie knew vaguely that he would have to do something about getting away but wasn't ready to think about it yet. They did discuss the possibility of being caught and decided that they would claim that Caril had been held hostage and knew nothing about the murders of her family members. Her later story was that Charlie had told her that her parents were being held hostage by a gang that was planning to rob a bank. She claimed not to remember anything about those six days.

Friends, employers, deliverymen, and relatives came by the house with increasing frequency. Charlie and Caril managed to send them all away, until the following Saturday, when Caril refused to let her older sister, Barbara, into the house. She followed the angry girl out to her car saying, "Just go home and don't come back till after Monday. If you do, things will happen—Mom will get hurt!" That night, Barbara's husband and Charlie's older brother, Rodney, called the police. The officers who came to the house believed the calm-appearing Caril's story that everything was fine, that the men had called the police in a family spat. They saw nothing to make them believe that anything might be wrong.

On Sunday, Guy Starkweather, Charlie's father, got into the act by sending Charlie's younger sister, Laveta, to see if she could discover what was happening. She returned with the story that Caril had whispered, "Some guy is back there with Chuck. He has a tommy gun. I think they're going to rob a bank." Laveta went and told Guy, but he did not act until the next day, when it was too late.

On Monday morning, Caril's grandmother knocked on the door and was refused entry. When she stormed off to the police, Charlie decided it was time to move . . . and quickly!

Running

They got Charlie's car from where he had left it the previous Tuesday and headed out of Lincoln toward the town of Bennet, to a farm belonging to August Meyer, where Charlie had often hunted. The smooth and dramatic James Dean–like flight that Charlie had envisioned was warped by bad tires, a sick transmission, and getting stuck in the mud at Meyer's farm. Charlie and Caril Ann agreed that Meyer ought to be shot for letting his road get in such bad condition.

They made their way through the cold to the farm, and within minutes the friendly old farmer was dead of a .410 shotgun blast that shredded his head. Dragging the farmer's body to an old washhouse and covering it with a blanket, they went into the main house and searched it. They took three guns, money, and some new clothes.

Working doggedly in the cold wind, they managed to dig their car out of the mud. Within minutes, however, it had slid off the road into a muddy ditch, and Charlie stripped the gears trying to get it out. A passing neighbor pulled the car out of the ditch, but the pair were seemingly reluctant to leave the area. They hung around a service station for a while, then returned to the road leading to the Meyer farm, only to get stuck in the mud again.

Despairing, they were heading for a storm cellar beneath an old, abandoned school when a car approached and Charlie decided that they should hitch a ride.

In the car were seventeen-year-old Robert Jensen, Jr., son of the general-store owner, and his fiancée, Carol King. They were the complete antithesis of Charlie and Caril. Wholesome, pride of the town, churchgoers, Bob and Carol might not have inhabited the same world as Charlie and his Caril. Bob, following the dictates of rural helpfulness, stopped the car and offered to help the pair. They asked for a ride to a phone. But as they drove, Bob made a comment about Charlie's "black Ford," as if he recognized Charlie, and the young killer began to fret that Jensen might turn him in. He put his gun against Jensen's head and ordered him to drive back to the storm cellar, while, at Caril's suggestion, he took what money Bob had in his wallet.

Charlie forced the couple down into the cellar, and, as they descended, he shot Bob Jensen in the head, six times. When Carol King screamed, he shot her, too. Or did he? Charlie later claimed that Caril thought he had raped Carol King and that Caril herself attacked and shot the girl in revenge. In fact, in an early confession he said that he had "screwed the shit out of that King girl." Later, however, he protested over and over that he had not harmed the girl sexually at all, but when her partially nude body was found, it was covered with blood. The body had a number of stab wounds in the groin area. One particularly brutal internal wound was made by an unusually shaped weapon that was never found. Later, in court, the sexual attack was never described. The prosecution chose to go after the pair only for Jensen's death in order to spare Carol King's family.

The two closed up the storm cellar and managed to free Bob Jensen's car from the mud. They drove back into Lincoln and past Caril's house, where they saw that the police were in possession. The remainder of the night was spent driving west, away from Lincoln, then turning around and heading back.

At dawn they hunted for a house to rob in the wealthy section of town, where Charlie had often collected garbage. They chose the home of C. Lauer Ward, an industrialist, and his wife, which was located only a short way from the garage where Charlie rented space to work on his car. The Wards' long-term live-in maid was present, but their fourteen-year-old son was away at school. The maid, who was deaf, saw Charlie at the back door and let him in. He entered with gun pointed.

Although they apparently had no real plan, the pair held the maid and Mrs. Ward hostage throughout the day, allowing Mrs. Ward to phone to cancel an appointment. They enjoyed eating quality food on request and generally lounged around, enjoying the feel of luxurious furniture that Charlie had never felt before and knew he would not experience again. In the afternoon, he allowed Mrs. Ward to go upstairs. But when he followed, she met him with a gun. Her shot missed and she ran. Charlie threw his knife at her, striking her in the back. While Caril guarded the maid, Charlie tied Mrs. Ward up, gagged her, and then killed her dog.

At some point during the day, Charlie and Caril composed a letter "for the law only," which was found in Charlie's pocket after they were caught. They also ransacked the house and took some clothing.

Lauer Ward arrived home at six, after a meeting with the governor of the state. Finding a runt-sized redhead holding a .22 on him, he fought for possession of the gun in a fight that took the men down into the basement. When Lauer tried to run back upstairs, Charlie shot him, too, in the back.

Charlie subsequently insisted that he had left the maid alive and unharmed, tied up upstairs, Mrs. Ward still alive on the bed, and Mr. Ward with only one bullet wound. However, when the bodies were found, all three had been stabbed to death. Charlie, who appeared to be surprised that the two women were dead, claimed that Caril must have done those murders. Caril, on the other hand, said that her lover had stabbed the maid to death.

The killers left the house in Mr. Ward's recent-model Packard and headed west once again. As they traveled, they wrote messages confessing to the murders they had committed and threw them out the window, though none was ever found. At one point they pulled off the road, made love, and slept for a short while before continuing on. Charlie blackened his distinctive hair with shoe polish. At 9:00 A.M. on Wednesday, January 29, they crossed the state line into Wyoming.

As they entered the town of Douglas, they heard on the radio that the Wards had been found and that the killers were traveling in a black Packard. Soon there were almost twelve hundred National Guardsmen, sheriff's deputies, state patrolmen, FBI agents, and others looking for the two teenagers.

Charlie determined to change cars somehow. West of town, they saw a car parked by the side of the road. Asleep in the front seat was Merle Collison, a thirty-seven-year-old salesman from Montana. Charlie, forsaking his quest for at least the appearance of self-defense, put seven bullets in the man. "Anyhow, whatever it was," he later said, "he would'a hated me if he had'a knowed me."

When Charlie started Collison's Buick, the emergency brake stuck. He was struggling with it when a helpful driver passed by, stopped, and asked if he could help. Joe Sprinkle, a geologist, saw the body in the car and grabbed at Charlie's gun. As he and Charlie were fighting for possession of it, a deputy sheriff drove by and stopped. A tearful, apparently frightened Caril Ann Fugate ran over to him shouting, "Help! It's Starkweather! He's going to kill me! He's crazy!"

Charlie escaped in the Packard, but a roadblock soon

caught him going about a hundred miles an hour. When a bullet went through the window by Charlie's ear and a splinter of glass cut it, he stopped his car and gave himself up. Among the few things Charlie said on the way to the sheriff's office was, "Don't be rough on the girl. She didn't have a thing to do with it."

Death Row

One of Charlie Starkweather's first acts in jail before he was transferred back to Nebraska was to write a letter to his parents. It said, among other things: "i'm sorry for what i did in a lot of ways cause i know i hurt everybody, and you and mon did all you could to rise me up right and you all ways help me when i got in bad with something But this time i would like you not to do any thing to help me out. . . . But dad i'm not real sorry for hwat I did cause for the first time me and Caril have more fun, she help me a lot . . ."

Although Wyoming wanted to prosecute Charlie and Caril for the murder of Merle Collison, that state had no capital punishment, and the courts concerned knew that the public must be satisfied. The pair were returned to Nebraska, where they could be executed. To the anger of the Starkweather family, including Charlie himself, the defense attorneys appointed by the court pleaded him not guilty by reason of insanity. At that point, the Starkweathers stopped helping the defense and gave their friendlier efforts to the prosecution. "Nobody remembers a crazy man," said Charlie to James Reinhardt.

It is probable that Charlie Starkweather suffered some

brain damage that could have played a role in his murder career. As a child he suffered a perforated eardrum, which could have indicated the presence of an infection that damaged the brain, and then he was struck on the head in his job at the newspaper warehouse. However, perhaps because he didn't want the public to think he was insane, he refused to have an electroencephalogram, which might have revealed such brain damage. He preferred to "burn."

Psychiatrists galore—in addition to Reinhardt—interviewed Charlie. Some he cooperated with, some he did not. Caril was never given any psychological testing, and, to this day, a number of years after she was released from prison, she remains an enigma. Unless she herself chooses to speak out—and it is unlikely that she will—there will be no firm answers to Caril Ann Fugate's participation in the murders. From the moment the sheriff's deputy came across them on the road in Wyoming, the two lovers who only wanted to be alone had nothing to do with each other. In fact, Caril forever after referred to "Chuck" only as "Charles Starkweather," as if he were a stranger who had accidentally popped up in her life.

Starkweather seemed to get a great deal of satisfaction from his position. He claimed that he had always wanted to be an outlaw, though he had not imagined that he would make it so big. He wrote a number of different confessions, though he never accepted any responsibility for what he did. The deaths all occurred, he insisted, as a result of "self-defense."

Caril and Charlie were tried separately, though only for

the death of young Robert Jensen. Because it involved a robbery (of the car and some money from his wallet), it was the most clear-cut case calling for the death penalty. And it was the clearest case in which Caril played an active role, by holding a gun on the youth while Chuck searched his wallet.

Charlie told Reinhardt: "I wanted [Caril] to see me going down shootin' it out and knowin' it was for her, for us . . ." As the date for his trial neared, however, Charlie wrote statements that put more and more of the blame on Caril Ann. Asked why, he replied, "I'll be convicted for what I didn't do." He told Reinhardt that he probably never really loved Caril, but liked the fact that she was willing to go "all the way" to death with him.

Charlie Starkweather was tried in May 1958. Each time he appeared in public, he maintained his I-don't-care, tousle-haired, drooping-cigarette look that sustained his carefully wrought teenage-rebel image. One psychiatrist noted that Charlie showed more interest in wearing the appropriate clothes to the trial than in its outcome. Another observed, "People don't mean anything to him. They are no more than a stick or a piece of wood to this boy."

Dr. John O'Hearne concluded, "Yes, he walks around in the body of a human being, but the thoughts and the feelings are not there like they are in an ordinary person, who has learned by being around others and has feelings for them, with them, and in relation to them. This is the way we learn to be people. I don't think he has ever learned to be a person."

Dr. John Steinman of Lincoln added that Charlie had no appreciation of human life. "He thinks he can feel close to certain people—he feels loyal and protective toward them—but he is incapable of feeling closeness with the depth and complexity of a fully developed human being. . . . I think he would be a child of five or six with a cap gun in a time of stress or strain with a gun. 'Bang, you're dead.' It means just about that much to him."

Charlie was found guilty and sentenced to die in the electric chair. All his father said was, "The Lord giveth and the Lord taketh away."

The following October, Charlie Starkweather testified at Caril Ann Fugate's trial, where she was tried as an adult. He was no longer feeling the least bit protective of her. The trait that had endeared her to him—her uncritical liking and approval of him—was a thing of the past, and so, now, he no longer attempted to keep her out of trouble.

She was the youngest girl in the history of America to be tried for first-degree murder. She pleaded innocent and claimed that she had been a hostage during the entire killing spree, but the evidence that she had had numerous opportunities to escape mounted up against her. She was found guilty and was sentenced to life in prison. In later years, a New York newspaper would call Caril Fugate a forerunner of female terrorists.

While Charlie was waiting for the death penalty to be carried out, he wrote his life story, in his own badly spelled, illiterate, but often compelling language. He hoped to get it published as a book, which he was certain that millions would buy. Part of it, cleaned up into blandness, was published in *Parade* magazine, but the remainder saw only what light psychiatrist James Reinhardt gave it in his book *The Murderous Trail of Charlie Starkweather.*

"Little Red" died in the electric chair on June 25, 1959. He was twenty years old.

7

He Wanted His Mother to Himself
Jack Graham

> We loved one another, but she wasn't a person you could call "mom."... You couldn't put your arms around her.
>
> Jack Graham to a psychiatrist

He knew from experience that it was quite possible that his mother would leave him and not come back. After all, that's what she had done when he was six years old. She left him in an institution and did not let him live with her again for five years. Now he was an adult, and he should have been able to deal with the fact that she was going away to his sister's just for a visit. But rather than take the chance that she would abandon him again, he killed her...along with forty-three other people on the airplane he bombed.

Thirty-year-old Daisy Graham of Colorado was on her second marriage—to a mining engineer much older than herself—when she gave birth to John Gilbert Graham in 1932. She didn't do much better on the second marriage than she had on the first. Her husband left her and her ten-year-old daughter, Helen, when Jack was eighteen months old. The three of them went to live with Daisy's mother, who could take care of the children while Daisy worked. His father, with whom he had no real connection, died when Jack was five.

Although the grandmother did most of the child tending, it was on his mother that little Jack focused most of his attention, mainly because she was so unpredictable. He never knew from one day to the next whether she was going to coldly reject him or shower him with gifts. But even the gifts weren't all that welcome, because any time he misbehaved she would point out how generous she had been as a way of increasing his guilt.

"You couldn't put your arms around her," he later told psychiatrists James A. V. Galvin and John M. MacDonald. "You couldn't show your affection like that to her. I don't know how to put it into words. . . . I always depended on her a lot. Everything had to be done exactly the way she wanted it. If she got mad at you, she'd stay mad for fifteen years."

That must be what Jack thought had happened after his grandmother died when he was six. Daisy stashed the children with a neighbor for a while, but that wasn't a permanent solution. Finally, unable to pay for child-care help, she sent Helen, now a teenager, to relatives and put little Jack in a state institution for boys without fathers. She had abandoned him emotionally all his life; now she was abandoning him physically, too. There was only one benefit—he had been a bed wetter since infancy, but he stopped as soon as he went to the orphanage.

When Jack Graham was nine, his mother married for a third time, to a well-to-do rancher named John Earl King. But now the certainty that he had been rejected by his mother could no longer be dismissed: she refused to let him leave the institution and come home to her. For the next two years, he only made trouble at the orphanage—fighting with the other children, taking things that didn't belong to him, losing what friends he had made by explosions of uncontrollable temper, and rarely seeing his mother. When he did get to visit her for vacations, Daisy used gifts as a substitute for hugs, but Jack knew the difference. He ran away from the orphanage several times, valiantly making his way to his stepfather's ranch, but Daisy—despite the disagreement of her husband—insisted that Jack be returned to the institution. What could he think except that his mother couldn't stand to be with him? But what he wanted most in life was to be with her.

Finally, at eleven, Jack was allowed to come to the new home to stay. . . or so he thought. As it turned out, his new home was so far into the mountains that in the winter he was unable to get to high school most of the time, and his stepfather made arrangements for him to stay at another ranch near the school, in return for helping on the ranch. So not only had he been sent away from home again, but he was so busy working that he had little time for the social activities that might have compensated. When he was at school he had to suffer being called "Abigail" by the students who found him just too different and too "secretive."

At fourteen, Jack left school and went to work full-time on his stepfather's ranch. However, prickly Jack was not the easiest boy to get along with. Used to being given gifts by his overgenerous mother, he saw no reason to put in a full day's work for a full day's pay, especially at his own home. So he was sent to a neighboring farm to work . . . and then to another. At each one, he invariably got into trouble, either with theft or violence. Within two years, all the ranchers in the area had hired Jack at one time or another and had had to fire him.

There was a perpetual layer of delinquency underlying Jack's life, though he was never arrested for anything. During one argument with his mother, he (accidentally?) knocked her down stairs. On another occasion, he may have set fire to an automotive garage that had refused him a discount. The cost of repairs was many tens of thousands of dollars.

The mountain-raised boy expressed interest in joining the U.S. Coast Guard and going to sea, but he was only sixteen. His mother went with him to the recruiting office to swear that he was eighteen. His six-foot height made the lie seem reasonable. On the surface it must have seemed that she was helping him, but underneath, he would have seen her willingness to lie in order for him to go away as another expression of her rejection of him.

While he was under arrest for murder, Jack claimed that he had tried to kill himself while in the Coast Guard because he had failed to hear from his mother for a long time, but the Coast Guard had no record of that. However that may be, the Coast Guard also rejected Jack within a very short time. He went AWOL and hitchhiked around the East Coast for forty-three days before being found and court-martialed.

"If I stay in the Coast Guard and don't get leave," he told an examining psychiatrist, "I'll go over the hill again to see my mother." Jack was honorably discharged as unsuitable to the Coast Guard when they discovered he wasn't of age. The official psychiatric report called him "an exceedingly immature individual who has exhibited poor judgment and who tends to act on impulses. . . . He is a dependent person, with strong ties to mother. He tolerates frustrations, even those in the normal course of work, very poorly."

He took that inability to tolerate frustration back into civilian life, where he proceeded to hold at least twenty-five different jobs, usually in construction work, in the next few years, both in the lower forty-eight states and in Alaska. Having learned early that he could get just about anything he asked for from his mother, he generally spent more than he earned, and in March 1951, having returned to Denver, he indulged in the most overt theft that he had yet attempted. While working briefly in a payroll office, he stole a stack of blank payroll checks, forged an executive's name, and cashed enough of them to buy a car and skedaddle.

Again wandering the western U.S.—cashing forged checks as he went—he worked many places before taking a job selling illegal liquor in Texas. He was arrested under an assumed name after trying to outrun the police at a roadblock. Sentenced to sixty days in jail, his real name was learned, as was the fact that Colorado had an outstanding warrant for his arrest for forgery. He was returned to his native state, where his mother and stepfather repaid most of the money he had stolen so that he could get probation instead of prison. The court required him to pay the remainder. Surprisingly, Jack Graham was very earnest in repaying the remainder of the debt on a strict payment schedule, and he also carefully fulfilled all the requirements of his probation.

The probable reason for his seriousness at that point in his life was that he had met a girl and, for the first time, fallen in love.

After his release from jail, at his mother's encouragement, he went to the University of Denver for some courses in business administration. There he met Gloria Elson. Immediately, he said later, "I wanted to put her up on a shelf and not let anyone else touch her or see her. I probably felt the same way as people do when they crave alcohol." Jack and the shy, serious girl were married in June 1953, when Jack was twenty-two. In less than two years, the couple had two children, a boy and a girl. Gloria had a very difficult, life-threatening time delivering the second child, so Jack, adoring her, promptly had himself sterilized so that she would never have to go through that again.

In October 1954, Jack's stepfather died, leaving Jack's mother almost a hundred thousand dollars. She immediately sought to entwine Jack again with her gifts. And even as he accepted them, Jack sought independence from her.

First, she insisted he return to the university. Then, she made the down payment on a house for him and his family—and his mother. Finally, thinking to make a good investment, she bought a drive-in restaurant in West Denver called the Crown-I, for him to run . . . with her help.

Living just with his wife and children, Jack Graham was able to be a mature, fairly responsible man, but the moment his mother moved into the house with them, he returned to his ambivalent dependence on her. It was exacerbated by the fact that the restaurant wasn't doing well. Whether or not she realized that part of the reason was Jack's continual dipping into the receipts, she tried to take control. Jack, angry at both her lack of trust and her challenge of his accounting, did not have the courage to stand up to her . . . or even realize that he could. His usual cheerfulness turned to moody depression.

Late that summer, in what he later called a suicide attempt, Jack abandoned a truck on a railway crossing, right in front of an oncoming train. The insurance company suspected that the claim was fake but was unable to prove it and had to pay up.

The following month, Jack caused a small natural-gas explosion at the restaurant, again in order to collect the insurance. He took that opportunity to close the restaurant for the winter. Whether it would ever have been reopened by Jack Graham cannot be known. The murder of forty-four people intervened.

The Bomb

Working nights as a mechanic, Jack had plenty of time to think about his situation. He gradually decided that, having gotten away with two fraudulent insurance claims, he would go for a big one by blowing up the restaurant. He surreptitiously went about collecting the dynamite, some special yellow electrical wire, the timer. He even took a part-time job with an electrician and worked with him long enough to learn how to do the wiring on a bomb.

Toward the end of October, Daisy King announced that she was going to leave Denver and spend some weeks in Alaska with Jack's older half-sister, Helen. Jack, feeling bereaved and rejected, tried to persuade her not to go. When she insisted on leaving, Jack tried to get her to at least wait until after Thanksgiving, but she said no, and purchased her airline tickets. The first stage of the journey was a United Airlines flight to Portland, Oregon, on November 1.

Excited at making the trip, Daisy prepared her bags, repeatedly changing her mind about what she could take. In the 1950s, aircraft passengers on domestic flights were not allowed to take more than sixty-six pounds of baggage without paying a premium for the extra. So she packed and repacked, always leaving room for the Christmas presents she would take to Alaska.

Jack changed the purpose of his homemade bomb. Instead of destroying the restaurant, he would take the opportunity to be free of his mother—who had had the nerve, once again, to let him know that he wasn't important!

He told his mother that he was going to give her a small hobbyist's electric drill for Christmas, so when his wife saw Jack put a wrapped package in one of his mother's suitcases, she assumed that it was the gift. She didn't see him hurriedly pull other presents for Helen's family out of the case to make room for the heavy package.

With all well on the surface, the family—grandmother, mother, father, hopping-skipping-laughing two-year-old boy, and tiny girl in arms—went to the airport to see grandma off. When grandma's luggage was weighed in, it was found to weigh one hundred and three pounds. The airline ticket agent suggested that Daisy remove some items and save herself twenty-seven dollars, but Jack quickly reminded her that, while in Alaska, she would need all the warm clothing she was carrying.

As Daisy paid the extra charge, Jack, apparently not even looking back at the bomb-laden suitcase being carried off, went to the insurance machines, where for a quarter a traveler could obtain a paid-up $6,250 policy that only needed to be signed. Jack pulled out the large supply of quarters he had brought with him and began feeding the machine. In his nervousness, he accidentally ruined two policies, one for $43,750 and one for $18,750. But he finally had two policies for $37,000 each, plus two more for $6,250. On the two smaller ones he put the names of his sister and an aunt. On the larger ones he wrote his own name.

Jack took the policies to his nervously excited mother to sign. Inadvertently she signed only three of them, omitting her signature on one of the large policies bearing his name as beneficiary. But Jack, busy checking on flight times, did not realize the error. Everything ready, he busily hugged her and helped her board the DC-6B that was being used for United Flight 629. As the plane was held up for a late passenger, the nervous tension of waiting, knowing that the timer on his homemade bomb was nearing zero, almost incapacitated him.

He stood with his family, watching through the large window, as the aircraft taxied down the runway, eleven minutes later than the schedule called for. Although Jack was aware only of his mother, there were forty-three other people on board: five crew members and thirty-eight other passengers.

As they watched, Gloria was not aware that anything was wrong with Jack, though the tension of waiting and the fear that the plane would not take off before the time set on the bomb's clock, were churning his stomach. When the little family went into the snack bar and ordered supper, before Jack could take one bite he had to dash for the men's room, where he was violently sick.

Eleven minutes out of the airport, at a few minutes after seven, the fragile four-engined Douglas aircraft exploded in midair. The wreckage and the bodies were strewn over an area eight miles wide.

The news reached the Denver airport while Jack and family were still eating. When the names of people on board were read aloud and Daisy King was among them, Jack collapsed into a chair, shaking and pale. He began to cry uncontrollably as Gloria took him and the children home.

During the following days, it was readily clear that the airplane had exploded because a bomb had gone off on board. A piece of a timing device and a section of yellow wire that did not match anything used on the aircraft were found on the ground below. The FBI became involved in every aspect of the investigation. They were prepared to scrutinize the private lives, friends, and finances of every single person on board.

Daisy King's purse, found in a field, was seen to contain an old newspaper clipping about her son, John Gilbert Graham, being sought by the police for forgery. Oddly enough, Daisy King was the only person to board the aircraft for the first time in Denver. Everyone else was on the way to Portland from somewhere else. It was also readily learned that John was the principal heir to Mrs. King's estate. His probably false insurance claims also came to light.

Graham did not know that he had come under scrutiny. Once he overcame the initial shock of what he had done, he began to make nervous references to the explosion. He talked about the explosion happening where it did and mentioned that if it had taken place a few minutes later, probably no one would have known that the airplane had been sabotaged. He described to a man he didn't even know the millions of tiny pieces the airplane must have been in after it blew up.

On November 10, less than two weeks after the explosion, the FBI, working through the list of personal interviews, reached Jack Graham. He quickly brought up his claim that his mother had ammunition packed in her bag, planning to do some hunting while in Alaska, a suggestion that was patently absurd. Three days later, the FBI agents returned to the Grahams' home and asked permission to search it. They immediately found a roll of wire matching the yellow wire used in the homemade bomb. They also found the presents that he had removed from his mother's suitcase to make room for the bomb.

Taken in for questioning, Jack held out until about midnight, when he finally said, "All right, what do you want me to tell you?" Three hours later he signed a confession and was formally arrested for sabotage, which did not carry the death penalty. The following day, the federal government relinquished him to the state of Colorado, and he was charged with the murder of his mother, for which he could be executed.

Jack Graham later repudiated his confession, claiming that he had made it because the FBI had threatened to arrest his wife. On December 9, he changed his plea from not guilty to not guilty by reason of insanity. After spending the following months in a mental hospital and being found sane, he stood trial while the nation watched on television. And in May 1956, Jack Graham was found guilty of murder and sentenced to die in the gas chamber.

All Graham said in explanation was, "She kept raising hell with me because I couldn't make the restaurant pay. It [had] been like that for six months. I had to do something." Yes, he wanted his freedom from his mother. But it was her leaving him, once again, when Jack desperately wanted her to stay, that had triggered Daisy King's death.

If he couldn't have her, no one could.

8

Aka Jesus Christ, the "Devil Doing the Devil's Work"
Charles Manson

> Charles Manson has a tremendous drive to call attention to himself. Generally he is unable to succeed in positive acts, therefore he often resorts to negative behavior to satisfy this drive.
>
> Annual report on prisoner Charles Manson

Even after being charged with the 1969 Tate-LaBianca murders, Charles Manson was revered by some as a hero of the counterculture. His "family," as his followers—mostly women—called themselves, were emotionally disturbed, drug-controlled dropouts who blindly accepted the semihypnotic leadership of the man they accepted as their "father," their "messiah."

Charles Milles Manson was born on November 12, 1934, in Cincinnati, Ohio, to a wild, unmarried sixteen-year-old named Kathleen Maddox. The young mother paid little attention to the fact of her unwanted offspring, gradually turning to prostitution and eventual imprisonment for five years for assault and robbery. She won a bastardy suit and support from a Kentuckian identified as "Colonel Scott," but she married a man named William Manson, staying with him only long enough to give Charlie a name. Some say his father was black, a circumstance that, if true, may have contributed toward Manson's hatred of blacks later in life.

During the first twelve years of young Charlie's life, he was shifted back and forth between neighbors, his grandmother, an aunt, and occasionally back to his mother, who took him west to Oregon, where there was another bunch of relatives on whom she could pawn him off. Torn by changing homes, lack of schooling, sojourns with an overly pious and strict aunt that alternated with a lackadaisical and mostly absent, alcoholic prostitute and criminal mother, Charlie became a confused and emotionally disturbed child.

At twelve years old, Charlie found himself living with his mother again, but this time, when she admitted she was unable to cope, she placed him in a state home for boys. The same procedure was repeated several times: his mother took him, then showed her rejection by placing him in a home; he escaped, he was caught, and the routine was started again. At thirteen, he finally managed to avoid capture. He was now on his own, starting a life of crime. Though he had an average IQ, he was functionally illiterate and he didn't care.

Along with another runaway, Charlie, with an almost

adult arrogance, was able to rent a room, which he used as a base for committing several burglaries. He was soon caught and, as the result of a mistaken idea that he was a Catholic, he was sent to Father Flanagan's Boys Town in Nebraska. Within just a few days, he and another boy stole a car and drove to Illinois. Again trying his hand at robbery—this time armed—Charlie was caught and sentenced to a reformatory in Indiana.

During the three years he spent in the reformatory, Charlie attempted to escape a dozen or more times. While there, however, he began to discover that it could be to his advantage to at least give the *appearance* of conforming to the rules. Manson, the con-man-in-the-making, was born.

Unable to see any long-term advantage in conforming, Charlie and several companions escaped in early 1951 and headed west, stealing cars and robbing gas stations along the way. Because transportation of vehicles across state lines is a federal offense, Charlie, when caught, entered the federal courts and prison system. In March 1951, at age sixteen, Charlie was sentenced to a federal reformatory in Washington, D.C., where he stayed until he reached his majority.

During those years in prison, Manson stopped growing, reaching an adult height of only five feet two inches. His natural belligerence increased as he decided, time after time, that he had to prove himself to anyone who challenged him. This, along with his inability to conform and accept authority in any form, set him apart. One psychiatric evaluation concluded that he was suffering from "a marked degree of rejection, instability and psychic trauma."

Resuming his conforming "con-man" persona, Charlie succeeded in getting himself transferred to a "better" reformatory in October 1951. But very shortly he was in trouble for sodomizing another inmate while threatening him with a razor blade, even though he had been about to be released in the custody of a willing aunt. Now labeled "dangerous," he was transferred to a more secure federal reformatory at Petersburg, Virginia, then to another, even more secure facility at Chillicothe, Ohio. The violence for which he would ultimately become known had begun for Charles Manson.

At Chillicothe, Charlie wised up. He decided not to fight the system but to use it. He worked when it would do him some good. He conned anyone he could to gain privileges and to further his own ends. Going to classes, he gained points as well as learning to read and becoming a proficient mechanic. Rewarded for good behavior, he was paroled in May 1954. He was nineteen.

Under the terms of his parole, Manson was allowed to go to Wheeling, West Virginia, to live with his mother. There he worked at several jobs and married a seventeen-year-old McMechan, West Virginia, girl, Rosalie Jean Willis, in January 1955. He tried, briefly, to lead a "normal" life, but couldn't hack it; it was just too dull, and it didn't give him any opportunity to experience the pleasure of feeling superior to others. He began stealing cars once again. When he and Rosalie drove a stolen car to California, they were caught. It was another federal rap for Charlie. But Charlie had learned other lessons well. He served as his own "jailhouse lawyer" and pleaded that he had been behind bars for so many years that he didn't know how to get along in the world. It paid off—he was given five years' probation—but he learned no real lesson.

Indicted in Florida, and again in the Midwest, he was taken back to California for parole violation and sentenced to three years at Terminal Island. For a while it looked as if he would earn time off for good behavior, but he made the mistake of trying to escape and found himself back in prison for the completion of his sentence.

Rosalie bore Charles Manson, Jr., while his father was in prison. His absence gave her the opportunity to realize that if she stayed with him, she would continue to suffer both physical and emotional abuse, so she filed for divorce and left the state. Charlie never saw his son and probably didn't care.

Charlie was released from jail in 1958 on probation. Ignoring the education he had so painstakingly acquired, he returned to petty thievery, auto theft, and various con games, as well as taking up a new activity, pimping. He had learned that he had the ability to charm women into doing as he asked. One girl in particular, called "Fat Flo," supported him with money from her parents. When he was charged with stealing and forging a U.S. Treasury check, he had one of his string of "girls" pretend to be pregnant, and talked the judge out of giving him a ten-year prison sentence. Despite the recommendations of both his parole officer and a court psychiatrist, who saw him as he really was—a psychopath, an incorrigible and confirmed criminal, and a danger to society—the judge gave in.

It is probable that during this period Manson was married again to a woman who bore him another son, but little is known about her. They were probably divorced in 1964.

Caught for violating the Mann Act (transporting a female across state lines for the purposes of prostitution), Manson had his parole revoked, and in 1960, at twenty-six, he was sentenced to serve ten years at McNeil Island Federal Prison in Washington State. At McNeil he honed his prison-learned skills of manipulating people to serve his own ends. He also became active in sports and learned to play the guitar, on which he saw himself as quite accomplished.

Since nothing middle-of-the-road suited Charles Manson, he began, while in prison, to explore different answers to "the meaning of life" and became particularly fascinated with Scientology. He claimed to have achieved the highest level, "theta clear," or, according to the cult's founder, L. Ron Hubbard, the level of "one who has straightened up this lifetime." Also reading about Buddhism, Manson selected those elements and concepts that met his own personal needs and feelings: "kama," "cease to exist," "coming to now," "reincarnation," etc. He interpreted them in his own style, one that he would later teach to his followers.

In 1964 his annual prisoner review stated: "[He]

remains emotionally insecure and tends to involve himself in various fanatical interests."

Then came the Beatles.

Manson did not just "like" the Beatles and their music—they became an obsession with him, an obsession of jealousy. He was convinced that his playing and the songs he composed were better than theirs. From 1964 to 1967, he composed almost a hundred different songs and played his guitar and the drums continually.

One friend and fellow inmate who also thought he was talented and helped him with the guitar, was lifer Alvin Karpis. The member of the infamous "Ma" Barker gang had recently been moved to McNeil Island from Alcatraz, where he had been imprisoned since 1934. He taught Manson to play the steel guitar and encouraged him to play professionally when he finally gained his freedom.

With his release imminent in 1967, Manson tried to persuade the authorities that he should stay; the prison was his home. He was afraid that he could not adjust to the world outside, where his genius might not be recognized. Now thirty-three, he had spent exactly half of his life behind bars. In most respects the prison authorities agreed with him—they too felt that his long record of criminality and instability would prevent him from functioning properly—in prison or out. One parole officer later said, "He told me right off there was no way he could keep the terms of his parole. He was headed back to the joint and there was no way out of it."

But the time had come, and even though he had no place to go, Manson was released on March 21, 1967.

Bearing an immense hatred for the establishment and considerable fear of the future, Manson headed for San Francisco, Berkeley, Haight-Ashbury, and the gathering of his "family" about him, and, ultimately, "helter-skelter."

Seeking Importance

Not knowing how to live a "normal" life, Charlie, released, set out to create his own institution—"the world according to Charles Manson."

The Manson "family" had its earliest beginnings in the revolutionary environment of the University of California at Berkeley and the free-wheeling and drug-infested Haight-Ashbury district in San Francisco. Moving into a rooming house near the campus in Berkeley, Charlie ignored his parole officer's advice to get a job and took to panhandling and playing his guitar for donations. It was in the Haight that he met Mary Brunner, a lonely, unattractive librarian who quickly succumbed to the strange attraction of the likewise unattractive Charlie Manson.

Mesmerized by Manson's special line of philosophical bullshit and his love-filled songs, Mary Brunner took him into her home and provided him with a place to live and financial support. In due course, Pied Piper Charlie brought in Lynette "Squeaky" Fromme to live with them, finding her on the day she ran away from her middle-class home. Soon, up to a dozen or more transient females—some no more than thirteen years old—were crashing with Charlie and Mary—in her pad and at her expense, and despite her objections.

Thus the Manson Family, with Mary Brunner the

charter member, was born. All willingly followed Charlie's strange preachings and songs of love, sharing, sex, and drug-inspired hallucination.

One of the mysteries about Charlie is the fact that young women were attracted to this singularly unattractive individual. Other than his brief marriage(s) and his almost as brief activity as a pimp, his primary sexual experience while in prison had been homosexual. Apparently, he offered, against a background of music, drugs, and sex, unqualified love and acceptance by another loser. Others who felt alone and alienated from the scorned "normal" world found themselves part of a family that they probably could have had in no other way. Though he claimed to be leading the women into liberation, he treated them as slaves—and they willingly did as he said . . . or left.

One thing that is certain—he did attract women as well as a few men, and used them unconditionally to build his private little universe. Charles Manson was "father" and supreme ruler, free to impose his own view of life on others.

In prison, Charlie had become a real actor. He could change moods from one minute to the next, as readily as he could change his hair styles. He could deliberately become Christlike in appearance and attitude and then the next minute change into the devil. He had a hypnotic way about him that could evoke any feeling he wanted in those around him. He had no fear of anything but was always alert to danger—a trait learned, he said, in prison. Viewing pictures of Charles Manson during these changeling years, one sees numerous different Mansons, from a completely normal-looking young male of the sixties to a Rasputinlike, wild-eyed fanatic.

As the decade of the sixties drew to an end, the way of life found in Haight-Ashbury had deteriorated into a bad scene of heavy drugs, sex, and crime. So Charlie and his family decided to acquire a bus and start traveling. Living by their wits and sharing money that came from new recruits and from relatives of Family members, they scrounged food and gas, stealing credit cards and generally eking out a living. Mary Brunner gave birth to Manson's son in a ritual that the entire Family celebrated. In 1968, the group ended up in the Los Angeles area.

Charlie continued to practice his musical skills and to develop his "teachings," which emphasized love, loss of self, freedom from fear of death, the sharing of all worldly possessions, distrust of the establishment, hatred of blacks, and acceptance of him as the "father," the "leader" who must be obeyed if a person was to stay in the Family. They shared everything, including their bodies, their minds, their possessions . . . and drugs. Everything he taught them served to erode whatever morals or inhibitions they had remaining. Theft, drugs, orgiastic sex, any perversion he could think of—they willingly indulged to gain a single approving glance from Manson.

Reaching Hollywood, Manson's initial goal was to be "discovered" as the latest star of the music world. To this end, he sought out and made friends with numerous top names in show business, including Dennis Wilson of the Beach Boys; Doris Day's son, Terry Melcher; and Gregg Jakobson, a top producer. They all recognized his talent and tried to help him, but he proved a most difficult subject. In the final analysis, his talent was insufficient to overcome his emotional instability, and they stopped working with him. Manson used this rejection to further his hatred of the "establishment."

Retreating from the Hollywood show-business scene, Charlie gravitated into the private world he was creating for himself and his followers. They found a base at the Spahn Movie Ranch near Chatsworth, about forty miles from Los Angeles. The ranch, owned by eighty-year-old, almost-blind George Spahn, was a rundown group of Old West–style buildings that had been used as movie sets for various western films. They conned old George into letting them stay there by lending Family member "Squeaky" Fromme to him as a housekeeper and "lover." It was at the ranch that a number of men joined the family or visited from time to time. It was also here that Charlie developed his image as "Jesus Christ" or God. He required the Family to act out a crucifixion scene in which they would erect a cross and tie Charlie-"Jesus Christ" to it. Of course Manson would come back to life, further emphasizing his "Christlike" nature and his immortality.

Charles "Tex" Watson became a devoted follower during this period, as did "Shorty" Shea, "Clem" Grogan, Bobby Beausoleil, Bruce Davis, and Juan Flynn. Manson also developed a working relationship with the Straight Satans motorcycle gang to acquire stolen cars and weapons. The Satans were paid off in part with sexual favors granted by female Family members at Manson's command.

The Manson Family's first known violence occurred as a result of drug dealing. A girlfriend of Tex Watson knew a black drug dealer named Bernard Crowe who was willing to make a buy. Tex and Charlie arranged for her to have Crowe bring $2,500 to a meeting, ostensibly to buy drugs, but in reality they would take the money from him. When they met, Crowe refused to turn over the money. Charlie pulled a gun and shot Crowe, leaving him for dead. Crowe recovered but was afraid to bring charges.

In another situation that developed at the ranch, Charlie and Shorty Shea got into an argument of sorts, after which Shea disappeared. Reports from various Family members later indicated that Charlie had killed Shea, dismembered his body, and buried the pieces around the ranch. The body was never found, but many of Shea's belongings, including a pair of matched pistols with which Shorty would not have willingly parted, were found in Charlie's possession or elsewhere on the ranch.

George Spahn began to get leery of the Manson group when there were several confrontations with the police. Then they tried to get him to make out a new will and sign the ranch over to the Family. Frightened, he ordered them off the ranch. However, they immediately found another house in Malibu canyon, where they lived while Manson's grand plan of "Helter Skelter" was germinating.

Meanwhile, carrying out his teachings, Manson would get the group loaded with drugs and play "games" in which they would simulate capturing and terrorizing a white person. Role playing, they would imagine how they would torture and terrorize their victim, enjoying their game all the while. He also taught them the technique of "creepy-crawly." This involved having Family members, dressed in black, break into homes of affluent white families at night. Without waking the residents, they would move furniture and otherwise disrupt the house before leaving as quietly as they had entered. These activities served both to frighten "whitey" and to provide further indoctrination into the crazy world of Charles Manson.

The final step that took Charlie Manson completely beyond the normal apparently took place following the publication of the *White Album* of the Beatles. This album, one of the group's most successful, carried very special messages to Charlie. He thought the Beatles were talking directly to him through the words of the various songs in the album as well as in other songs they recorded. (The Beatles vehemently denied injecting any meanings beyond the obvious into their songs, and they at no time had any intention of inspiring violent actions by anyone.)

Charlie and the Family played all the Beatle music frequently, interpreting the words their own way. The end result was Charles Manson's culminating philosophy ...*Helter Skelter.*

To Charlie, Helter Skelter meant the coming, world-wide revolution in which the black race and the white race would engage in wholesale warfare. The blacks would "rise" and exterminate the white race. That is, all except the Manson Family, which would escape to a "bottomless pit" in the desert near Death Valley. There they would find safety in a beautiful land of milk and honey beneath the desert floor, where they would live in love and peace and multiply.

Drawing on certain passages in the Book of Revelations in the Bible, and utilizing the number twelve times twelve that appears there, Manson anticipated that his Family would, over the years, increase to 144,000 people. By that time, the black race, unable to rule itself, would be in turmoil, ready for a complete takeover by the Manson Family. Charles himself would return as king—a second "Jesus Christ."

Although the words *helter skelter* as used in the Beatles' song probably referred to an amusement-park ride in England, Charlie thought that its references to ups and downs meant the rise of the black race and the fall of "whitey." Similarly, he thought the "coon" in "Rocky Raccoon" referred to the black man. Every possible wording in other songs that would support Helter Skelter and the impending Apocalypse were interpreted accordingly by Charlie.

Charlie didn't just dream. He set up bases in the desert in the Panamint Mountains near Death Valley, where the Family would ultimately find "the bottomless pit" for their escape. About two hundred miles from Los Angeles, near Inyo, California, the Family occupied two properties known as the Myers Ranch and the Barker Ranch. At these locations and in the desert nearby, they cached quantities of weapons, dune buggies, and other supplies to be used to fight their way to the hole in the desert and their "promised land."

But Helter Skelter wasn't happening fast enough for Charlie's satisfaction, so he decided to hurry it along. What better way than to commit a series of violent murders of "whitey" that would appear to have been committed by "blackie." And so he set Helter Skelter in motion on July 29, 1969, with the murder of Gary Hinman.

The Murders and the Murderers

Members of the Family, others who knew Charles Manson, and various officials later suggested that he was responsible for up to thirty-five murders. More realistic figures indicate that the number of killings he committed or inspired was somewhat less. Whatever the number, Charles Manson was a psychopath with absolutely no conscience, no regrets, no respect for life, a hatred for "the establishment," and a lust for his own sexual satisfaction and the fulfillment of his messianic complexes. He was tried and found guilty of the premeditated murders of eight people in three specific cases.

The Gary Hinman Murder

Gary Hinman was a musician and a friend of both Manson and another family member, Bobby Beausoleil. He was murdered by Beausoleil under orders from Manson.

Robert Kenneth Beausoleil, aka "Cupid," twenty-two, was a movie bit player who, although a Family member, would come and go from time to time, though he was completely under Manson's spell.

Hearing that Hinman had come into a lot of money, Manson decided that he should have it to further finance Helter Skelter. On July 25, 1969, Manson gave Bobby, Susan "Sexy Sadie" Atkins, and Mary Brunner a gun and some knives and told them to go to Hinman's Malibu home and get the money.

The threesome dropped in on Gary Hinman "just to visit and chat." When Gary said he didn't have any money, Bobby pistol-whipped and beat him, to no avail. So Bobby called Charlie. Charlie and Bruce Davis then drove to Malibu and confronted Gary.

Bruce McGregor Davis, twenty-six, was already a hardened criminal. He did yeoman service in stealing jeeps and dune buggies and acquiring stolen credit cards and guns. He hung around for the drugs and sex as much as for any belief in Charlie's preachings.

Following further beatings and denials, Charlie cut Gary badly with a favorite knife he had brought along, nearly severing an ear. Charlie and Bruce then left. After another day of torture and threats, Bobby called for more instructions. Charlie said, "Kill him!" Loyally, Bobby stabbed Gary Hinman to death while the girls watched. Following instructions from Manson, they painted the words POLITICAL PIGGY and a large paw print on the walls in an attempt to implicate the Black Panthers and initiate the racial revolution predicted by Manson.

Bobby and the girls cleaned up after their murderous task was completed but failed to clean off all their fingerprints. Taking two of Gary's cars, which he had signed over to them, they headed back to the ranch. The first Helter Skelter murder was now history.

A few days later, Bobby was apprehended while driving one of Hinman's cars, and the police found the murder weapon in the car. Based on fingerprints found at the crime scene and evidence provided by Bobby's girlfriend, Kitty Lutesinger, Susan was also charged with the Hinman murder and was locked up in the Sybil Brand Institute to await trial. Bobby was charged with murder, and subsequently Charlie, Mary Brunner, and Bruce Davis were also implicated and charged.

The Tate Murders

With Helter Skelter finally under way, in the early evening of Friday, August 8, 1969, Manson called together Family members Tex Watson, Susan Atkins, Leslie Van Houton, Patricia Krenwinkel, and Linda Kasabian to give them their instructions. "Now is the time for Helter Skelter."

Fortified with drugs and armed with a gun, knives, rope, and wire cutters, they were to take one of the Family cars and go to 10050 Cielo Drive in Beverly Hills. That was the former residence of Terry Melcher and Candice Bergen. Manson thought that Melcher had betrayed him, and so did not care who currently lived in the house. They were to break in, murder everyone present, steal what cash they could, and make the murders as gruesome as possible, along with making it look as if the murders had been committed by blacks.

Charles "Tex" Watson, twenty-three, was originally an "all-American" boy from Copeville, Texas, raised in a typical God-fearing Christian family. He attended the Methodist Church, was a Boy Scout and a Future Farmer of America, and was successful in school activities. However, while in college, beer, sex, and visions of a different life started to take over. He dropped out and moved to California, where he reveled in the availability of liquor, sex, and drugs.

Tex met Manson at the home of Dennis Wilson, one of the Beach Boys singing group. As he wandered through the various rooms of the mansion, partaking of the drug-filled atmosphere, there was Charlie, playing his guitar to a bevy of entranced young girls. As Tex listened and watched, Manson seemed to exude an aura of love and peace, and the room was filled with a gentleness and a serenity that Watson had never felt before.

The bearded, diminutive creature with a guitar had hooked another apostle.

A song of Charlie's said, "Cease to exist, come to say you love me." He preached that one should kill one's ego, die, give one's self over completely to the total love, the total togetherness that could be found with Charlie and Family. Tex succumbed and gave himself and all of his possessions to Charlie in the late spring of 1969.

The relationship culminated on the night of August 8, 1969, when Charles Manson asked . . . when he *ordered* Tex Watson and three of the Manson girls to go commit murder at 10050 Cielo Drive and then again at the LaBianca residence.

Charles Watson had fallen so far under the mesmeric influence of Charles Manson, and had lost his feeling of self so completely, that he did not hesitate to murder at Manson's command. A short time after the murders had taken place, Manson threatened Tex with a knife and asked, "Will you die for me?" Tex answered, "Sure, Charlie, you can kill me!"

The murder team, drugged to the hilt, did their job all too well. After cutting telephone wires to the house, they gained access to the property by scaling fences, careful not to set off alarms. Their first victim was an innocent bystander, young Steve Parent, who had been visiting the caretaker, William Garretson, who was in his apartment over the garage, listening to his stereo with headphones on, unaware of the murders happening just yards away. Parent was stopped by Watson just as he was about to open the electric gates to leave. Tex shot him dead, and the group proceeded into the house.

There they found movie star Sharon Tate, who was the very pregnant wife of director Roman Polanski; Hollywood hairdresser Jay Sebring; coffee heiress Abigail Folger; and her friend Voytek Frykowski. Within minutes, they had carried out Manson's instructions to the extreme. Each of the four victims in the house was either shot or stabbed, as many as forty or fifty times, and left to die in their own blood, which was used to write the word PIG on the front door.

Linda Kasabian, called "Yana the Witch," who eventually became a prosecution witness, had remained outside as lookout and, urging the others to stop, had not participated in any of the killings. Both Susan Atkins and Patricia Krenwinkel entered into the blood-letting, torturing and stabbing their victims until the very end.

Susan Denise Atkins, aka Sadie Mae Glutz, twenty-one, first made contact with Charles Manson in Haight-Ashbury, where she had lived the drug-and-sex-filled life of the stereotypical flower child. Arrested on felony charges at least once, she spent three months in jail before meeting Charlie. She was also involved with Satanism. Charlie readily took advantage of her sexual promiscuity to lend her to others when he needed things from them.

In court, Susan described her first meeting with Charlie, when she had heard him singing "like an angel": "When he was through singing, I wanted to get some attention from him, and I asked him if I could play his guitar . . . and he handed me the guitar and I thought, 'I can't play this,' and then he looked at me and said, 'You can play that if you want to.' . . . It blew my mind, because he was inside my head, and I knew at that time that he was something that I had been looking for . . . and I went down and kissed his feet."

Following the Tate-LaBianca murders, Susan was arrested and held in the Sybil Brand Institute awaiting trial. While there, she talked freely to her cellmates about her role in all three of the murder cases, describing her actions and feelings with enthusiasm and great detail. The roommates told the authorities, and much of Susie's casual chatter was used against the Family in court. "You have to have a real love in your heart to do this for people," she said of killing Sharon Tate, an act which she described as sending "a rush" through her. Then she said of the act of murder, "The more you do it, the better you like it."

Patricia Krenwinkel, aka Katie, twenty-one, unlike some of the Manson girls, was not very attractive and, according to some of the Family men and visiting bikers, "was too hairy." However, she was one of Charlie's favorites and often had sex with him to the exclusion of the others. Already a minor criminal when Charlie found her, she was a devoted follower and believed in Charlie completely. She even came to believe that he had the power to work miracles, and testified that she had seen him do it.

After leaving the Cielo Drive house, the murderers changed into clean clothes and discarded their blood-stained garments along the roadside. They stopped on their way back to the ranch to use the hose of a nearby residence to wash the blood from their hands and faces. Although the homeowner almost apprehended them, he, luckily for him, was unable to stop them. However, he obtained their license number as they made their way back to report the night's happenings to their "father," their "God," Charlie Manson.

The tally for the evening—seventy dollars in cash, no valuables, just five human lives snuffed out in the most senseless and brutal manner, all on the whim of a madman.

A maid found the bodies the next day. Sharon Tate had been stabbed sixteen times, Jay Sebring seven times as well as shot, Abigail Folger twenty-eight times, and

Frykowski, fifty-one times; he also suffered five gun shots and a dozen or more blows to the head.

The LaBianca Murders

After returning to the Spahn Movie Ranch early on Saturday morning, August 9, the murderers found Charlie dancing naked in the moonlight with one of the girls. His first questions were, "Why are you back so soon?" and "Why didn't you go to any other houses?" He asked how they felt, did they have any remorse, did they feel any guilt? All replied in the negative and then went to bed as if to rest after a hard day's work.

Later that day, after listening to news of the murders on the radio, Charlie called the murderers together again and said he had another job for them, but this time "not so messy." Steve "Clem" Grogan and Leslie Van Houton were to go with them. They all gasped as Charlie said that he himself would lead them.

Leslie Van Houton, aka LuLu, twenty, was, of all the Manson girls, the most beautiful. She played the role of a "little mountain girl," complete with accent, and pretended to be afraid of everything about her. She probably feared Charlie a great deal, but in the end would always obey and comply with his every wish. When discussing the Manson Family with the prosecution, she said, "You couldn't meet a nicer group of people."

Steve Grogan, aka Clem, seventeen, was, according to some, a "certified idiot." An escapee from a mental hospital and severely retarded, he joined the Family early and became Charlie's pet. Charlie told everyone in the

Family that they should be more like Clem because he was as innocent as a little child. He needed no deprogramming and accepted the Manson teachings blindly. Of all the Manson Family members convicted of murder, Clem was the only one who probably should have been found innocent by reason of insanity.

So, late on Saturday, August 9, the seven Family members started out in search of victims but with no one particular in mind. After selecting a likely house in Pasadena, Charlie walked around the property but rejected it when he saw pictures of children in the house. After all, he loved little children.

After rejecting several other houses, they finally selected a large Spanish-style house at 3301 Waverly Drive, near Griffith Park in the Los Feliz section of Los Angeles. It just happened to be next door to a house Charlie had once visited and not enjoyed. After checking the house from the outside, Charlie and Tex entered through an unlocked door, where they confronted Leno LaBianca, a wealthy supermarket owner, and his wife, Rosemary. Armed with a gun and bayonet, Charlie and Tex tied them up and told them not to worry—"We won't harm you. All we want is money."

Upset with the small amount of cash found in the house, a disappointed Charlie and Tex gagged the LaBiancas with pillow cases and called Katie and Leslie to come into the house. Charlie then decided to leave, but only after telling Tex to let the girls do some of the work—both of them. The LaBiancas were in hysterics, trying to scream and break loose, as Charlie and the others departed, leaving Katie, Leslie, and Tex.

The girls took Rosemary LaBianca into the bedroom where Tex "went to work" on her with the bayonet. Then, remembering Charlie's instructions to make things as gruesome as possible, Tex and the girls mutilated both victims. Tex carved WAR on LaBianca's belly, and, even though the victims were probably already dead, the girls stabbed both victims repeatedly, using kitchen knives and heavy cooking forks and leaving a fork and a knife stuck in their bodies. Again, following Charlie's instructions, they painted the words RISE, DEATH TO PIGS and a misspelled HEALTER SKELTER in the victims' blood on the walls and appliances in the house.

Even with the carnage around them, they washed up, prepared a meal, and fed the family dogs before leaving and hitchhiking back to the ranch.

After Charlie and the others left the LaBianca murder scene, he had attempted to find a friend of Linda's who was to have been another victim, but they were unable to locate her. So another day of Helter Skelter had ended. The Family awaited the coming days with excitement, certain that the great black versus white war was about to begin.

Aftermath

A few days after the murders, the police raided the Spahn Movie Ranch on a warrant concerning stolen cars. The Family—the police counted twenty-six people living there—had been stealing Volkswagens to convert into dune buggies. They were all released, however, when it turned out that the warrant was wrongly dated, and nothing more was done in the matter. Manson moved his Family to the Barker Ranch in Death Valley.

The major brouhaha concerning the star-studded murders insisted that the Cielo Drive house had been the scene of massive drug-driven orgies, that all stars had to be concerned for their lives, and that Roman Polanski was looking for publicity (he quietly volunteered to take a polygraph test). Everyone—from mystic Peter Hurkos to Truman Capote, author of *In Cold Blood*—offered an opinion.

Nothing more happened in August. In September, Roman Polanski offered a reward for information. In October, the police raided the Barker Ranch with warrants charging Manson with numerous felonies unrelated to murder. While they were there, two young members of the Family, seventeen-year-old Kitty Lutesinger, who was pregnant with Bobby Beausoleil's child, and Stephanie Schram, fled into the arms of the officers asking for protection. And they began to talk.

Bit by bit, the mysteries started to unravel. First Susan Atkins was arrested for the murder of Gary Hinman. A compulsive talker, she began to tell her tale to her roommates at the women's house of detention. From numerous directions (some of which were not linked up for many months because so many jurisdictions were involved), information began to gather into one horrifying picture. Finally, at the beginning of December, Manson and his Family were arrested for murder.

The main trial, that involving Charles Manson, Susan Atkins, Patricia Krenwinkel, and Leslie Van Houton, for the murders of the seven Tate-LaBianca victims (Tex Watson and the others were tried separately), lasted over six months and was the longest and most expensive criminal trial held in the United States up to that time. The problems involved were horrendous. Not only did the prosecution have to provide the evidence, both real and circumstantial, that the accused were actually guilty of the crimes, but they had to provide the motives. With Vincent Bugliosi, deputy district attorney of Los Angeles, heading the prosecution, over forty law enforcement officers from at least four different government agencies and jurisdictions were involved in searching out, investigating, and presenting hundreds of pieces of evidence and hundreds of witnesses.

The primary witness was Linda Kasabian, who, at twenty-one, had already been married twice and borne two children, when she met Charles Manson. She testified for eighteen days, telling incredible, chilling details about life in the Family, while those members on trial threatened her with death if she kept on talking.

Likewise, the accused, although represented by up to sixteen different attorneys at different times, and presenting great difficulties by their lack of cooperation and their disruptive tactics, were given every opportunity to present vast quantities of evidence, counterevidence, and witnesses on their behalf.

The judge and the jury operated under great duress at all times during the trial due to the erratic and sometimes violent conduct of the defendants, the obstructionist tactics of their attorneys, and even the threat of physical violence.

The trials provided a media circus and received local, national, and even worldwide coverage beyond all reason. Family members who had not been indicted held a constant vigil outside the courthouse during the entire trial. One of the girls incised an X into her forehead with a hot screwdriver because, she said, that was what was being done to her "father."

The night before the defense was to begin, Manson told his attorneys that he had ordered the girls to confess to the killings and take all the blame. The girls' attorneys refused to let them do so, and the next morning the attorneys rested the defense, with no witnesses called at all. The girls objected, and finally Manson said that he would testify.

"I have stayed in jail and I have stayed stupid and I have stayed a child while I have watched your world grow up. . . . Most of the people you call the family were just people that you did not want, people that were alongside the road; I took them up on my garbage dump and I told them this: that in love there is no wrong."

Later he reverted to his childhood: "I don't care what you do with me. I have always been in your cell. When you were out riding your bicycle, I was sitting in your cell looking out the window and looking at pictures in magazines and wishing I could go to the high school and go to the prom. . . . My father is the jailhouse. My father is your system. . . . I am only what you made me. I am only a reflection of you." On concluding, he ordered his codefendants not to testify, and so the defense closed its case.

While awaiting trial, during the trial, and even after Manson's conviction and imprisonment, the Family continued to exist and to commit numerous violent and criminal acts, still orchestrated by remote control, through their blind faith and belief in their "lost leader."

Charles Manson, Susan Atkins, Patricia Krenwinkel, and Leslie Van Houton were found guilty of the Tate-LaBianca murders and sentenced to death. Manson, Bruce Davis, Bobby Beausoleil, and Clem Grogan were found guilty of the murders of Gary Hinman and Donald Shea, even though Shea's body was never found. Squeaky Fromme, tried separately, was acquitted, but was later sentenced to life in prison for trying to assassinate President Gerald Ford. Tex Watson fought extradition from Texas for many months, managed to get himself found to be insane, and then was finally tried for murder and found guilty. All of the death penalties were commuted in 1972 to life in prison by the U.S. Supreme Court decision against the death penalty.

In an interview with *Life* magazine, years after Manson went to prison, "Jesus Christ" said, "Hey, time and circumstance made me into this Manson guy. Satan. Society wanted to buy this evil, mass-murderer–devil–fiend. I'm nobody. I'm the last hobo in line. Give me a bottle of wine and put me on a train. . . . I don't fit in the world that you guys live in, so I live over here in the shadows of it."

PART IV

DEMONS
STRANGLEHOLD ON A MIND

Ancient peoples believed firmly that evil spirits could take possession of humans' bodies and force them to do things that they would not normally do. These spirits, generally thought to be under the control of a major evil figure, Satan, were responsible for most of the bad things that people did. In the fifteenth, sixteenth, and seventeenth centuries, it became the work of "witch hunters" to seek out those people who were possessed and destroy them in order to defeat Satan and to save their souls. For the most part, any person who suffered from a mental illness was viewed as being possessed.

Most of us do not believe in such demons and possession these days, but failing to believe in something does not necessarily mean that it does not exist.

In recent years, two prominent murderers have professed that they were taken over by demons, who forced them to carry out their gory deeds. David Berkowitz, the "Son of Sam," killed six women and maimed nine more young people at, he said, the demand of demon dogs. Ronald DeFeo, on the other hand, did not know what possessed him to kill his parents and four brothers and sisters. He just knew that his personality had changed after he moved into the house in Amityville. . . .

"I Had No Choice.
I Had to Do It"
Ronald DeFeo

I'm not sure if I'm Ronald DeFeo sometimes.
Ronald DeFeo, Jr., after the murders
of six other family members

An average Brooklyn family sought the privileged life of
the suburbs of Long Island and found that their lives
began to change . . . as if there were something malignant
in their beautiful Amityville house. Whatever force was
there culminated in the murders of six members of the
family by the seventh. But who or what was controlling
his hand—his own mental quirks or an evil force that had
been part of the land for generations?

It began with Amityville itself, on the south shore of
Long Island, a short drive from Brooklyn. Long ago, a
small tribe of Indians buried their chief, a tall man

with a distinctively underslung jaw, in the position reserved for special people—standing up in the grave. In the late 1700s, when settlers arrived in the area, a farmer digging a well for his cattle accidentally exposed the skeleton of the Indian. The farmer's young son, enraptured by his first sight of a skull, took the bony structure with its peculiarly underslung jaw and carried it to the newly built house, where he spent long hours playing with it, as if it were a toy. He often placed a candle inside it and rode around the neighborhood in darkness, trying to scare people with the lighted skull.

The spirit of one of the Indian chief's avid followers, enraged by the liberties taken by the boy with his hero's skull, took revenge on the boy, who died when his pony fell on him after trying to jump a fence. Thereafter, any young male who lived in the location of the old burial ground was vulnerable to haunting by the Indian.

This information about the Indian chief and his follower came through Mrs. Ethel Johnson Myers, a medium used by psychic investigator Hans Holzer, when she went into a trance in the house at 112 Ocean Avenue in Amityville in early 1977, more than two years after the vicious murders of the DeFeo family.

"The whole atmosphere," she said, from the depths of her trance, "people get to fighting with each other because they don't know why. They're driven to it because they are taken over by the one with the long jaw."

The first house built on the site was moved in 1928 to another location in Amityville. There are no records as to why the house was moved, but perhaps the inhabitants came to recognize that the house itself was not the problem, but the location of it. The large, three-story, Dutch Colonial house that was, most unusually for the waterfront neighborhood, built at right angles on the lot, developed a long tradition of tragedy. The house called "High Hopes," with its oceanfront position, boathouse, and swimming pool, became the proud possession of the DeFeo family in 1965.

Ronald, Jr., called Butch, was thirteen when he moved with his parents and three younger brothers and sisters (a fourth was born soon after moving) out of their Brooklyn apartment to the pleasant suburb, which didn't necessarily enjoy having the loud, violent, showy family as neighbors. Butch's father, Ronald, Sr., service manager of a major Buick dealership in Brooklyn that belonged to his father-in-law, wanted all things wonderful for his children and gave them pretty much everything they ever asked for. But he and his oldest son also gave each other a lot of grief. Young DeFeo told Hans Holzer from Dannemora Prison that he was aware of a personality change in himself after he moved into the house, that he became "cold and vicious inside" but deliberately showed the image of "a coward" to other people.

Mr. DeFeo brought his own violent personality with him from Brooklyn. He demanded that his son be the strong older son that is often expected in an Italian family, and Butch, who was downright fat as a teenager, was unable to live up to DeFeo's expectations. DeFeo most often tried to reinforce his expectations by striking his son. But then he would turn around and give him anything he wanted—such as a four-thousand-dollar speedboat when the boy was only fourteen.

Soon after the family moved to Amityville, Butch's grandparents were staying in the house and he used a particularly foul word about his grandfather. The old man took off his belt to beat Ronnie with it. Butch retaliated by throwing furniture at the old man. When his grandfather chased him, Butch ran. He crashed into Dawn, the sister closest to his age, and began beating her with his fists. Butch was taken to a psychiatrist who soon recognized that the boy was terrified of his father and in serious need of some way to relieve the feelings that he normally kept stuffed down with food.

The powerfully built father and his fat son were at loggerheads most of the time, especially after Butch got thrown out of school after school, usually for insolence and physical violence (although he took pride in never hitting a nun at the Catholic schools he usually attended). The first time Butch was expelled from a school, his father knocked his front teeth out and ranted that he had only married his mother because she was pregnant with Butch.

Eventually Butch left the Catholic school system and went to Amityville High School, where he began to use drugs. He said in court, "I couldn't take living in my house, and I felt if I had to live in my house I had to do something about it. So, to take my mind off it, I used drugs." Butch finally left school at sixteen without having graduated.

* * *

The Growing Tension

He then proceeded to get thrown out of job after job—or at least he left before he actually got fired, most often for just not showing up. He finally went to "work" at his grandfather's car dealership as a mechanic and general helper. There he didn't have to show up if he didn't feel like it. Taking full advantage of what he regarded as the privileges of being the manager's son, he often did not show up at all.

Otherwise, Butch drank, wandered around, used drugs, and hunted girls, whom he would sometimes sneak into a small, finished, concealed room in the basement of the house for a tryst more comfortable than the backseat of a car. In his late teens he began to use drugs to get some of the gross fat off his body, and from then on, though still quite husky for a man only five feet eight inches tall, his endless supplies of money and a certain amount of physical attraction brought him a steady stream of girlfriends.

In 1972, when Butch was twenty-one, a man he had met in a bar was found drowned in the canal by Ocean Avenue. Missing from his pockets were the more than two hundred dollars he had borrowed that day. According to Gerard Sullivan, the man who later prosecuted him for murder, some Amityville police officers thought that Butch DeFeo may have had something to do with the death and theft, but he never came to official attention for the deed.

One of Butch DeFeo's hobbies was guns, and he collected good-quality rifles when he could talk his father out of the money. That wasn't always necessary, however, because he also had become a thief, stealing outboard motors off boats anchored along the canal that led to the ocean and reselling them. One police officer warned him that he was going to be caught, and when, in fact, he was, Butch threatened the policeman's daughter's life. The threat, reported to his father, resulted in another of the many parent–son blowups. Butch, tried for the theft, was put on probation for a year.

In 1973, Butch happened to have a rifle in his hand when his father was being particularly abusive. The young man aimed the rifle at his father's head and pulled the trigger. By some miracle, the gun failed to go off. It was then that his psychiatrist told Butch that he belonged in a mental institution. That statement only contributed to the growing paranoia the youth was experiencing, convinced that everyone was out to get him in some way.

While the episode had the effect of turning Butch more paranoid, it made his father turn to religion. DeFeo brought a Canadian priest to stay in the house for a while, though Butch had abruptly left, unable to deal with the thought of a priest in the house . . . or perhaps forced out by his demon. The elder DeFeo acquired, and had Butch install, a number of religious statues that he placed around the grounds of the house. He often went out to the largest shrine on the front lawn to kneel in front of it and say the rosary.

Several times Butch, who had come to feel like a stranger in his own family, tried to leave home. On one occasion he got a girlfriend to claim to be pregnant so that they would have to get married. His father bought off the girl by paying for the abortion she didn't need and forcing his son to return home. Another time, his father took his son's car from the apartment where he was staying, forcing him to return home to get it. Each time Butch tried to leave and become independent, his father would bribe him with whatever the young man wanted most at the time. His father said, "I'll give you all the money you want. All I want you to do is live in this house." Butch did not have the guts to say no and mean it.

"I knew some day it was going to come to a head," he told Holzer, "either he was going to kill me or I was going to kill him. I knew this was coming, and he knew it was coming, and it was no secret from anybody."

In the summer of 1974, things were coming to a head between Ronnie DeFeo and his family. The tension was so great that he was having trouble indulging in his favorite pastime of sex with the women he knew. He tried to leave home—again—and failed—again—despite the fact that he told his father—and anyone else who would listen—"I'm going to kill you if I stay here." His father merely reiterated that if Butch left home, he would get no more money of any kind from his family.

When asked later if he still loved his family at that point, he replied, "Yes, sir. I didn't want to kill them. To be quite honest about it, it's not that I wanted to do it, I had no choice. I had to do it."

* * *

The Demon Kills

On November 12, a Tuesday, Butch failed to go to work at his grandfather's Buick dealership because he had a stomach ache, a symptom of stress that frequently plagued him. He and his father had had one of their physical confrontations the previous day, and he had a swollen upper lip and some bruises—another reason for not going to work.

He slept late and then hung around the house for the rest of the day. He didn't eat dinner with his family because he didn't like the brown "shit in a bowl" that his mother had prepared. Instead, he watched TV in the small lounge on the second floor, from which he heard his sister Dawn in a major brawl with his father. She came storming by muttering about killing everyone in the house. Later, as he continued to watch TV, he heard the other members of the family chatting quietly together, and the demon within him began to suspect that they were conspiring to harm him.

"We'll wait until he goes to sleep" and then get him, he was certain that he heard the others say.

Continuing to watch television, he became as absorbed as he could in a violent war movie called *Castle Keep*. "As absorbed as he could" because part of his mind was surely being consumed by the idea that, as in the movie, he should take care of his enemies by violence.

And who were his enemies? His family, of course—starting with his father.

At about 3:00 A.M., with the lights glaring in the house, twenty-two-year-old Ronald DeFeo, Jr.—or some-

thing that had taken possession of his body and mind—
put the family sheepdog outdoors, where it proceeded to
bark for the next fifteen minutes. Then he grabbed his
expensive .35-caliber Marlin rifle and crept into his
parents' bedroom. He fired two shots at his sleeping
father's back, and then, as his mother, Louise DeFeo,
awoke and started to rise, he fired two more shots at her.
His father probably lived long enough to move around
somewhat in the bed before dying.

The young man who had never done anything calmly
in his life calmly moved on to thirteen-year-old Allison's
room. She, too, looked into the muzzle of the gun with
sleepy eyes, only to have a bullet smash her face and
enter her brain, destroying it. Crossing the hall to the
bedroom of his youngest brothers, twelve-year-old Mark
and seven-year-old John Matthew, Butch stood between
the twin beds and fired first at one, then the other, from
less than two feet away. It's likely that Mark, who had
been seriously injured in a football accident and could
not turn over of his own accord, was turned onto his
stomach after death.

As the heavyset young man reloaded his rifle while
climbing the stairs to the third floor where his sister
Dawn slept, the eighteen-year-old probably woke up. It is
also likely that brother and sister spoke together, with
him calming her fears enough to send her crawling back
into bed before he shot her at the base of her skull. Oddly
enough, investigators found unburned gunpowder parti-
cles on her nightgown, which may indicate that Dawn
herself had fired a gun. One of the stories that DeFeo told

after he was arrested was that Dawn had killed their siblings after he had killed his parents and before he killed her, but there was no other evidence that this might have been the case. DeFeo did, however, confess later to an incestuous sexual relationship with his sister.

Going into the bathroom he shared with Dawn, DeFeo promptly threw up in reaction to what he had done, then took a shower and got dressed in his normal work clothing. Because of the usual DeFeo confusion about key rings, he grabbed the first ring he found that had a key to his car, not realizing that it had no house key. He left the house, took time to throw the rifle into the mouth of a canal entering the ocean, and drove into Brooklyn to the car dealership on Coney Island Avenue. It was still not even dawn, so he went to an all-night diner and hung out until the service department was opened.

Butch's father was not expected at the agency that day because he was scheduled to take young Mark to the doctor. Junior hung around the place, running a few errands, and making frequent phone calls to his house, but there was never any answer, which he commented on in puzzled tones to anyone within earshot.

Leaving at noon, Butch spent the afternoon chatting with friends, drinking in bars, wandering a shopping mall with a casual girlfriend, and phoning home, making more and more to-do about the fact that no one answered. One friend he met told him that there were two cars in his driveway, so someone must be home. Toward the dinner hour, he stopped at the house of one of his heroin suppliers and got a fix. Finally, leaving friends in a bar, he said he was going home to break a window in order to get in. He returned minutes later to announce that his parents had been shot.

Within a few hours, the police of Amityville knew they had a horrifyingly major mass murder on their hands. The crying Butch DeFeo, soul survivor of the massacre of his family, voluntarily went to police headquarters to give whatever information he could, which consisted primarily of suggesting that a syndicate-related acquaintance of the family might be responsible. The policemen he worked with appreciated his cooperation.

But in the meantime, other policemen were discovering more accurate information, information that led them to ask Butch more questions. Bit by bit, in trying to explain the discrepancies they found in his story, he began to admit that things had not been completely hunky-dory in the DeFeo home. Finally, about thirty-six hours after the murders, Ronald DeFeo, Jr., admitted that he had killed his parents and four brothers and sisters.

"It all started so fast," he said quietly. "Once I started, I just couldn't stop. It went so fast."

He freely confessed in vile language that indicated only hatred and contempt for his victims, referring, for example, to his sister Dawn as "that fat fuck." He then voluntarily signed the more sedately worded written confession.

Within days, however, DeFeo was saying that he did not, in fact, remember actually killing his family, though he would accept that he had because the evidence seemed to indicate that. What he remembered was that he fell asleep in the TV room and was awakened by his sister, who handed him the .35-caliber Marlin rifle. In all calmness, he went to his parents' room to kill them while she killed their two brothers and sister. Ronnie noted, in puzzlement, that the gun "didn't make any noise" when it went off. He cleaned up the shell casings left on the bedroom floors. Then, feeling certain that Dawn would turn on him next, he shot her, too.

Soon after that, he told an investigating psychiatrist: "I'm not sure if I'm Ronald DeFeo sometimes."

After being found legally sane and able to stand trial, Ronald Joseph DeFeo, Jr., was tried in September 1975, in a proceeding that lasted nine weeks. His only real defense was insanity, which could not stand up against the prosecution witnesses who testified to hearing him threaten to kill his father just a few days before he did so.

At the hearing to determine whether the original confession should be suppressed, DeFeo's grandfather testified. Finishing, he asked the court's permission to kiss his grandson. Given the nod, Mike Brigante approached the well-dressed, bearded defendant and whispered to him, "Tell him the truth and the truth shall set you free." Many of those standing near as the old man kissed the young man who had murdered his daughter heard Butch DeFeo reply, "The truth will get me life."

The prosecution revealed a spoiled kid who, seeing his gravy train getting slower, and having increasingly violent reactions to the vicissitudes of his life, lashed out with a rifle. Butch himself tried his hardest to appear to be insane on the witness stand, and a very reputable psychiatrist (who would later testify in the David Berkowitz case) stated that he found him to be a paranoid psychotic, but the jury did not buy it. They regarded Butch's statement that he had heard voices in his head telling him to kill as just more evidence that he was playing at appearing to be insane. The jury ignored the improbability of a person shooting six people in a quiet house and not trying to get away. After deliberating for three days, the jury found Ronald DeFeo guilty of six second-degree murders. He was sentenced to serve six consecutive terms of twenty-five years to life for the murders.

The Demon House

With DeFeo tucked away in prison (while his conviction was being appealed), the house on Ocean Avenue in Amityville went on the market. Very few people, knowing its history, were interested, until George Lee Lutz (called Lee), a land-survey-company owner from nearby Deer Park, and his wife found it to be the house that fulfilled all their dreams. They could afford it if they moved the business into the house along with their three children by Kathy's previous marriage.

On December 18, 1975, thirteen months after the murders, the Lutzes moved into the house. A priest from a nearby Long Island parish arrived at their request to bless the house. As he began his ritual, he heard an unknown voice order him to get out. He proceeded with the blessing, but warned the family not to let their children sleep in a certain room—later determined to be

Butch DeFeo's bedroom. Later that day the priest was seen to have almost black circles under his eyes that had certainly not been there earlier. During the following weeks, he experienced strange illnesses that could not be adequately explained.

In *The Amityville Horror*, published in 1977 and written with Lee Lutz, author Jay Anson tells the story of the twenty-eight days following the Lutzes' move. Supernatural beings who possessed the house gradually drove the family almost berserk and did drive them to leave the house, abandoning all their belongings. They experienced weird temperature changes and objects moving apparently of their own accord. Most mornings, Lee awoke at 3:15, the hour of the DeFeo murders, and was unable to return to sleep. His daughter Missy befriended a pig-faced demon whom she named Jodie. Both Kathy and Lee became virtually unable to leave the house, so that at Christmas the family had very few presents. Huge clusters of dead flies accumulated at certain windows—when there had been no sign of a fly in the rooms.

The most gruesome phenomenon occurred late one night when George tried to wake Kathy, but as he watched she turned into an old, old decrepit woman. It took several hours for the horrifying change to wear off. One acquaintance of the family who was known to be psychic visited the house and informed the Lutzes that it was haunted by the spirits of people who had died in their sleep and did not know that they had died. He gave the family simple instructions on procedures to follow to let the ghosts out of the house and go on their way. But the phenomena did not end.

Perhaps the most important change was that Lee went through some personality changes that caused him to neglect his work. Severe migraine headaches, which he had never before experienced, attacked him for days at a time. Eventually, he came close to losing his land-surveying business. After the family fled the house the night of January 14, George sold his business and the family moved to California.

(Later books reveal that the "Entity" went to California with the Lutz family and continued to pursue them for a number of years. The author of the later books, John G. Jones, wrote that the land where the DeFeo house was located had, since time immemorial, been known to the Indian inhabitants as a place of evil. In a later time, an escapee from the Salem Witch Trials lived there and continued to practice his evil arts.)

The news of the Lutzes' experiences burst into the public media, and lawyers, psychiatrists, and journalists began to review Ronald DeFeo's words in terms of "the Amityville Horror." Hans Holzer was contacted to investigate the house for Butch's attorneys. On January 13, 1977, he went to the now-empty house with the medium Ethel Johnson Myers (who did not know what house they were visiting) and a photographer known for her ability to capture psychic phenomena on film.

Holzer followed Mrs. Myers around as she tried to find a good place to settle in the empty house, to enter a trance. He filmed her until his camera inexplicably stopped functioning. The psychic photographer, however, was able to take a number of Polaroid pictures in the bedrooms that revealed aural lights around the approximate spots where Butch's bullets had entered the bodies of his siblings and parents.

Mrs. Myers was able to feel the presence of an ancient Indian burial ground and the anger of the Indians that still existed at the site—"When they are very mad everybody goes crazy," she said. This was particularly true of white men, it seems, because the Indian chief with the underslung jaw had, after his skull was played with by a white boy, cursed any white people who might live in the house.

But, she added later, "Who's going to believe that a psychic force has taken over an individual in order to make them commit such atrocities?"

The jury didn't, but much of the public has come to accept just that. After another family lived in the house at 112 Ocean Avenue in Amityville and left after two years, it was bought to be opened as a tourist attraction.

10

"I Want My Soul Back!"
David Berkowitz—
The Son of Sam

I am tormented
I cry in my cell
I miss my Daddy
I hate myself
I am very uptight
I hear demons
I see demons
I need to talk to someone
I cannot be left alone
I will have a breakdown
I cannot be understood
I am truthful
I am doomed
    From the writings of David Berkowitz in prison

First it was the voices. They sent him out, looking for blood. Then it was dogs. He suddenly knew that they were demons set to watch him. Their howling—which no one else heard—was the howling of devils demanding blood and death. Then he saw a specific dog, a black labrador owned by Sam Carr, who lived down the street from David's Yonkers, New York, apartment. Sam, the demon in the dog, demanded that he kill young women. David Berkowitz became the Son of Sam, and the Son of Sam killed.

"Dad, the World Is Getting Dark Now"

David Berkowitz was always a loner, convinced that the world did not notice him...or, if it did, that it actively hated him. The chubby child's only technique for dealing with his peers was to be a bully. Those people who knew him had two views of young David: sometimes he was docile, polite, willing; other times, especially after he learned at age seven that he was adopted, he was the stereotypical bully—hostile, destructive, and frequently truant. Though he knew he was different from everyone else, involvement with his adoptive mother and father kept him from turning too much into himself as he was growing up. However, in 1967, when he was thirteen, his mother, Pearl, died of cancer, leaving him alone with his father, Nat Berkowitz, the adoptive parent to whom he felt least close.

Until 1971, David lived with his father, who then remarried. Smarting at what seemed to him to be deliberate abandonment, David joined the army, became a sharpshooter, and served in Korea. Apparently he was no better at making friends in the military than he had been at school. During that period, the New York Jew converted and became a Baptist. After completing his enlistment at Fort Knox, Kentucky, David was discharged in the summer of 1974 and returned to New York to live with his father and stepmother.

Some months later, Nat, disgusted at having his hardware store robbed, retired and moved to Florida. Twenty-one-year-old David remained behind, alone— and lonely— in New York City. There were few influences to keep the "good" David to the forefront—his inability to make contact with other people made certain of that.

Soon after he moved into his own apartment, Berkowitz started to be aware of the dogs. He was certain they were demons determined to torment him with their howls, viciousness, and slavering. On March 2, 1975, he killed a German shepherd with a shotgun. He knew that it was not a dog but a demon come to torment him . . . and that it had to die.

For a short while David's life changed in a way that had the potential to stop the demons, but in the long run, the change was only brief. David located his real mother, Betty Falco, who, eighteen years before, had given her son, fathered by a married man with whom she had a long-lasting relationship, up for adoption. She was overjoyed to meet her son, as was David's half-sister Roslyn, who was fifteen years older than he. For a while he became an integral part of a family, but his demons would not let him stay. By the time he killed for the first time the following year, he had stopped visiting his mother and sister.

As the months passed, David endured growing loneliness. His work consisted of a nighttime guard job—alone, except occasionally when he worked, ironically enough, with guard dogs. His days consisted of more isolation, because he deliberately shut himself into his small apartment and saw no one.

It is probable that during those long months, David's insanity was developing along lines that would lead to murder. After he was arrested, police found in his apartment several notebooks filled with notes on almost fifteen hundred fires that he may have set in a period of little more than a year. He was never charged with setting any of the fires because none had caused a death. However, fire-setting has long been recognized as one of the precursors of serial murder, almost as if it were practice in not caring what happens to anyone else.

In November 1975 he wrote to his father: "Dad, the world is getting dark now. I can feel it more and more. The people, they are developing a hatred for me. . . . Many of them want to kill me. I don't even know these people, but they still hate me. . . ."

He chose to brood on that perceived hatred. Taking a leave of absence from his job, he incarcerated himself in his small Bronx apartment, covered the windows, and stayed completely without human contact for almost a month, his only friend the perpetual practice of masturbation.

He emerged from that isolation a killer.

* * *

The Quest for Prey

On Christmas Eve 1975, he went hunting someone to kill, carrying only a hunting knife. He went to Co-op City, the huge development where he had previously lived with his father. He drove through the streets that defined the many high rises making up the complex, looking for a woman alone. Voices within him said "Her!" when he saw a woman coming from a grocery store. He leaped from his car, drove his knife into the woman's back, and then was horrified when she began to scream. The voices had not prepared him for so much noise.

"I wasn't going to rob her, or touch her, or rape her. I just wanted to kill her," he later said, still puzzled that the woman—who was never identified—had screamed so.

Running away among the buildings where he had grown up, still driven by demon voices demanding blood, he came across a fifteen-year-old school girl. He stabbed again and again at Michelle Forman's head and back. Again his victim screamed, again he ran off.

Somehow, drawing blood, even though the victim lived, released Berkowitz from his desperate need for isolation. He returned to work, but he started hunting for another place to live, a place—he hoped—where the demon voices would not find him. He moved in with a family in Yonkers. But they had a large dog, one that howled, though not nearly as much as the howling that David heard in his head all day long. Unable to sleep, getting tireder and tireder, David decided, then, that the dog was a demon. And the demon was after him.

Soon after beginning work for the U.S. Postal Service in March 1976, David Berkowitz moved again, away from the demon-dog, he thought. This time he moved into an apartment building. Though his rooms overlooked only the Hudson River and the Palisades, he was certain that he was being watched, and so he nailed blankets over the windows. Within days, however, he was aware of another dog, this one belonging to a man named Sam Carr who lived in a house across the street from David's apartment. And that dog, too, was a demon, a six-thousand-year-old demon that David came to know as Sam.

David tried to destroy the demon-dog by throwing a Molotov cocktail into the yard, but he only succeeded in calling fire trucks to the area.

" 'Sam' Was Relieved"

The demons were demanding blood again, but Berkowitz knew that the knife was not the answer. Though he didn't understand why, it set women screaming, and it even caused blood to spew across the wielder. Looking for an alternative, he went south to visit his father in Florida and then to see an army acquaintance in Houston, Texas. There he acquired a Bulldog .44 pistol, the weapon that would at first make him known to the public as the ".44-caliber killer."

Late on July 28, 1976, back in New York and working as an air-conditioner installer, David Berkowitz took his

Bulldog and, responding to the demon screams in his head for blood, went hunting.

At one in the morning, Donna Lauria, an eighteen-year-old emergency medical technician who had been to a relative's wake with her family, and Jody Valenti, a nineteen-year-old student nurse, were talking in Donna's car, which was double-parked on the street in front of her Bronx home. Dave, seeing the pretty dark-haired girl behind the wheel, parked his own car and walked back, Bulldog .44 in a paper bag in his hand. Unknowing, the girls chatted on . . . until bullets crashed through the window. One struck Donna in the neck, killing her quickly. Another penetrated Jody's thigh, sending her diving for the car horn.

Driven away by the noise, David ran to his car and drove home. The feeling that "Sam" was pleased sent the howling of the demons into abeyance, and he slept in peace. That feeling was to stay with him for several weeks, satisfying his need to kill. He claimed later that Sam, the Prince of Darkness, had promised Donna Lauria to him in marriage at some future time when she would arise from the dead.

The peace brought to David by the killing did not last, however. When he continued to have severe headaches, his mother, following the idea of Nat Berkowitz, who was concerned at long distance about his son's complaints, suggested that David see a psychiatrist. David, however, refused to get help. He was too far away from reality and into being a tool of Satan.

On October 19, an anxious, pacing David Berkowitz

was driven out into the night again by the howling of the demons demanding a woman's blood. Seeing two young, long-haired figures in a car parked in Flushing, he shot through the window. The bullets missed Rosemary Keenan, a student at Queens College and the daughter of a policeman, but struck twenty-year-old Carl Denaro in the back of the head. He recovered after surgery.

Perhaps because no one had died, David found no real peace after the shooting. On Thanksgiving he visited his mother, but the next night, November 26, he attacked again. Again late at night, again in Queens, but this time not through a car window. Sixteen-year-old Donna DeMasi and her friend Joanne Lomino, two years older, went to a movie and returned home by bus about midnight. David, heeding the commands of his demons, followed them toward Joanne's house. As they frantically tried to escape the echoing footsteps and unlock the door, he fired directly at the two girls. As they fell, he elatedly emptied his gun at the house.

Donna, shot through the neck, would recover. Joanne, taking a bullet in her spine, was paralyzed for life. David had done dreadful damage, but again he had failed to kill.

On Christmas Eve, a year after his first attack on a woman, David killed one of the demon-dogs, a German shepherd that lived on Wicker Street, not far from the Carr house. The demons were not happy.

A month later, on January 29, 1977, he got a chance to redeem himself. Unable to sleep, he set out on the prowl, again going to Queens. As he walked around Forest Hills, his inner demons ordered him to kill the young woman he saw getting into a car with her boyfriend. Ignoring the man, John Diel, David put two .44 bullets through the car window into Christine Freund and had the satisfaction of hearing the demons' voices go silent. Twenty-six-year-old Christine died several hours later with one bullet in the temple and one in the neck.

It was at that time that David Berkowitz saw himself as being responsible for keeping the whole world safe. He knew—positively *knew!*—that if he did not provide blood when the demons demanded it, Sam would take revenge. "Once I remember his demons were howling all night long and I didn't do anything. The next day there was an earthquake." Earlier, he was reluctant to interact with other people. Now, he was completely unable to—it wasn't safe!

On the early spring evening of March 2, Berkowitz, unable to resist the howling, even though it was several hours earlier than he usually went out, returned to Forest Hills. There, on a street near the famed West Side Tennis Club, he encountered Virginia Voskerichian, a twenty-one-year-old who had come from Bulgaria as a child. The attractive Barnard student, returning home late from classes, was met by a single bullet in the face, a single bullet that killed her instantly.

By this time, the police had put together the different attacks involving a .44 pistol and knew that they were probably hunting for one man. They announced a special task force to hunt for the killer of Donna Lauria, Christine Freund, and Virginia Voskerichian. Operation Omega was headed by Captain Joseph Borrelli. David delighted in the fact that the world was watching, though he objected to the press coverage given Borrelli's comment that the killer must hate women.

On April 17, David went on the prowl again. Before he reached Queens, he was stopped by police officers and cited for driving without current car insurance. Remaining in the Bronx, he spent long hours cruising the city, waiting for the targets that he knew would satisfy the demons' lust. Finally, about three in the morning, only a few blocks from where Donna Lauria had died, he found eighteen-year-old Valentina Suriani and her twenty-year-old boyfriend, Alexander Esau. They had just returned from a show and late dinner in Manhattan, and were embracing when David fired four shots through the car window. This time, both Valentina and Alex died.

David was carrying with him a letter he had meticulously printed—though with some misspellings—and addressed to Captain Borrelli. He dropped it in the road near the death car, where the first officers on the scene found it.

Dear Captain Joseph Borrelli:

I am deeply hurt by you calling me a wemon hater. I am not. But I am a monster. I am the ''Son of Sam.'' I am a little brat. . . .

I feel like an outsider. I am on a different wavelength then everybody else—programmed too kill.

However, to stop me you must kill me. Attention all police: Shoot me first—shoot to kill or else keep out of my way or you will die!...

I am the "Monster"—"Beelzebub"—the chubby behemouth.

I love to hunt. Prowling the streets looking for fair game—tasty meat. The wemon of Queens are prettyist of all. I must be the water they drink. I live for the hunt—my life. Blood for papa...."

And so the ".44-caliber killer" became the "Son of Sam."

Son of Sam's next victim was "Sam" himself—the black labrador that belonged to Sam Carr. The yard where he lived could be seen from David's apartment, but only David heard him howling every day. Before the Suriani and Esau slayings, Dave wrote an anonymous letter to Sam Carr, complaining about the dog. Two days after the deaths, he wrote again, ending with these words: "I have nothing to lose anymore. I can see that there shall be no peace in my life, or my famlies life until I end yours." Eight days later, David shot the black lab. The dog survived, but the bullet in its side was in such a position that it could never be removed.

As the press took up the story of the Son of Sam in

ever larger headlines, columnist Jimmy Breslin challenged the killer to give up. David sent a reply that was published in the *Daily News*. It included the following:

> Don't think that because you haven't heard from me for a while that I went to sleep. No, rather, I am still here, like a spirit roaming the night. Thirsty, hungry, seldom stopping to rest; anxious to please Sam.
>
> Sam's a thirsty lad. He won't let me stop killing until he gets his fill of blood.

And he reminded Breslin to "Remember Ms. Lauria," the anniversary of whose death was coming up.

Not until June 25 did David Berkowitz go out to kill again. It was a hot night, with his apartment made even more stifling by the blankets he always kept pinned over his windows. He drove the streets until he decided to park near a disco in Bayside. Judy Placido, who had just graduated from high school, had met Sal Lupo at the disco. It was almost surprising that she had met anyone, because the crowds were thin now as New York City gathered fear of the Son of Sam about itself. But she and Sal had become acquainted and he offered to drive her home. They had just shut themselves in Sal's friend's red Cadillac when the killer they had been discussing fired through the window. Judy took bullets in her spine, her neck, and her temple, but by some miracle none of them did any permanent damage. Sal took a bullet in the arm. Berkowitz was puzzled that the attack failed to kill.

He did not know that the name David Berkowitz had finally come before the Yonkers police. Sam Carr had given them the name as one of several possible people who might have shot his dog. But the hundreds of men and women working on Operation Omega had no reason yet to connect that name with their manhunt.

On Saturday, July 30, David once again found the weather sweltering. He took his car and drove and drove. It was not until two o'clock in the morning, in Brooklyn, after long hours of prowling the streets, that he parked by a fire hydrant and left the car. A policeman saw the illegally parked car and ticketed it while David watched from a distance. The demons drew David to a lovers' lane, where a number of cars were parked, most with couples in them. He saw one flash of long, gleaming-brown hair and headed toward that car, but as he reached it the driver pulled away, only to park farther down the road. David, reluctant to follow, remained where he was in the shadows, and soon the empty spot was filled by the car belonging to twenty-year-old Bobby Violante. Stacy Moskowitz, also twenty, was with him. The pair had met just a couple of days before at a restaurant and were on their first date.

David watched the couple leave their car to play on the nearby swings for a few minutes. The howling in his head grew louder. He watched while they returned to the car, which was parked under a bright streetlight, and made themselves comfortable in each other's arms. And the howling said, "Kill."

"I knew I'd have to go through with it this time. I didn't care if anyone saw me. It didn't matter, I had to shoot them."

Tommy Zaino, the young man in the car that had moved forward, saw David move toward Violante's car, step into the street while pulling a gun from his belt, and fire through the window. The police finally had a witness.

Two .44 bullets struck Bobby Violante in the face, destroying one eye and leaving only twenty percent vision in the other. Other bullets hit Stacy in the head; she died a day and a half later. David ran off, back to his ticketed car. He drove the remainder of the night, then sat in a park until far into the daylight hours.

As the police worked frantically on every lead, a pair of Yonkers detectives began to wonder about Son of Sam's letter to Jimmy Breslin. There had been an apparently meaningless reference to "Wicked King Wicker." One dog had been killed on Wicker Street. There was another reference to John Wheaties; Sam Carr, whose dog had also been shot, had a daughter named Wheat. None of that meant anything, but they began to look more closely at Carr's list of possibles, which included David Berkowitz.

At that same time, the man who lived under David Berkowitz's apartment became another victim, of sorts. The killer, seeing Craig Glassman as another demon—in fact, as the master of demons and therefore *his* master—had set a fire containing cartridges at Glassman's front door. Calling the police, Glassman also gave them some curious anonymous letters he had received. They contained a reference to "Captain Carr," and Berkowitz had written, "I am the killer, but Craig, the killings are at your command . . ." The Yonkers police sent their information to the Operation Omega task force.

Ending in Sight

David knew that the end was nearing for him . . . but the demons didn't care. They only wanted more blood, and he was failing to give it to them.

A woman who had been walking her dog near lovers' lane the night Stacy and Bobby were shot reported that she had spotted a strange-looking young man awkwardly holding something up his sleeve that might have been a gun. Remembering too that she had seen a police officer writing tickets in the area at approximately the same time, she finally gave the detectives something concrete to go on. They found that a summons had been written for David Berkowitz. Calling Yonkers, they learned about the dog-killing strangeness in which he was involved.

The link was finally made. Many officers prepared to be in at the arrest of David Berkowitz at his Yonkers apartment.

On August 10, 1977, a Wednesday, David's demons drove him to place every weapon he owned in his car, although, he said later, he did not feel as if the demons were going to demand that he kill that night. Two men, sent to investigate the fact that Berkowitz had received a summons the night of the Moskowitz murder, saw his car and discovered that he had a machine gun in the back seat. That was all they needed to make an immediate arrest. But the order to take him did not come through; they were waiting for a search warrant . . . and waiting.

Not until ten o'clock did David Berkowitz emerge from his apartment. The hidden police recognized that he carried a gun in a brown paper bag tucked into his left hand. They let him get into the front seat of the gun-laden car, then arrested him. David Berkowitz just smiled.

"It had to come to an end. They had used me, the demons. They always used people. Now they'd have to find someone else to do those things. I was happy it was over."

David Berkowitz was indicted for five murders and six attempted murders. The first psychiatrists who worked with Berkowitz determined that he was unfit to stand trial. But the prosecutors of the Son of Sam knew that the public would never accept a plea of insanity from the man who had kept their city on tenterhooks of fear for a year. By New York law, he could be out on the streets again in a year. The Kings County district attorney retained Dr. David Abrahamsen to examine Berkowitz for the prosecution. Abrahamsen, a forensic psychiatrist of international renown, reached the conclusion that, "While the defendant shows paranoid traits, they do not interfere with his fitness to stand trial."

By the time the trial came around in May 1978, however, Berkowitz was saying that he would plead guilty to second-degree murder. The original judge, John Starkey, told the press that he would refuse to accept a guilty plea if Berkowitz continued to talk about demons. Starkey was removed from the case, primarily because of the inadvisability of talking openly to the press.

By that time, even the psychiatrists who had earlier found him incompetent, decided, on reexamination, that he was fit to plead. At the time of sentencing, he put on a display of insanity, shouting, "Stacy is a whore! Stacy is a whore!" Dr. Abrahamsen saw this as a "carefully orchestrated effort in avoiding the sentencing." But he could not avoid it. David Berkowitz was sentenced to a number of consecutive terms in prison, adding up to 547 years. His story of killing at the demand of Satan would never come out in court.

The following February, the "Son of Sam" announced to the press that he had invented the demons, that it was all "a hoax, well planned and thought out." He then wrote to Dr. Abrahamsen, starting a correspondence and series of visits that ultimately produced Abrahamsen's book, *Confessions of Son of Sam*. In it, the psychiatrist thoroughly investigated David Berkowitz's own view of his background and came to see him as an isolated, unloved psychopath, who, having never matured sexually, came to blame women for his own inadequacies, and who killed with "clear-headed cunning."

David watched young couples in sexual situations, fantasized that he was participating, and then did participate by shooting a gun instead of an erect penis, thus not having to be rebuffed. In addition, couples making love in cars are apt to produce babies, unwanted babies such as he was. The woman he was shooting was always his natural mother. The command of the "demons," Abrahamsen wrote in *The New York Times*, was "a command dictated by strong, repressed sexual urges."

Berkowitz admitted to Abrahamsen that he had indeed set numerous fires. The psychiatrist realized that the only period in which David wasn't busy setting fires was during the months when he was looking for his mother. He says, "This gave him sufficient sexual satisfaction to refrain from pyromania."

Berkowitz told the doctor that he could not stand loud noises, whether the barking of dogs or the blasting of nearby TV sets. Abrahamsen said that it was this sensitivity to noise that led to his story of the demon howling that drove and drove him to murder.

Abrahamsen's analysis is thorough and detailed, with numerous examples of the double personality that ultimately became, as the psychiatrist described it, the gentle, pleasant, helpful David Berkowitz versus the cunning, criminal, murderous Son of Sam.

The demon story does not die, however—not even with Berkowitz. In 1981, Terry Maury published "news" articles in which he suggested that the Son of Sam's murders had been carried out by Berkowitz at the command of the leader of a cult. David did not deny it; instead, he freely said that, indeed, there had been several cult members with him on each murder.

So what is the true story of David Berkowitz, Son of Sam? Which story is one to believe? Which one does David himself believe? Or is there another story that David will tell some day, when the demons urge him to?

PART V

INJURY
THE VIOLENT BRAIN

Logic tells us that if something is wrong with the brain itself, physically, that is, that if the brain is injured, something will change in the way we think or behave.

Dorothy Otnow Lewis, professor of psychiatry at the New York University School of Medicine, found that most juvenile delinquents who have killed were physically abused as children. And there is a higher proportion of violence among those children who had suffered head injuries than among those who hadn't.

Head injuries or lesions that bring violence to the fore tend to be those that impinge on the limbic system, the most ancient part of the brain, where aggression originates and from which it can overwhelm the controls that the "civilized" mind has placed over it.

One of the most memorable explosions of violence that may have been caused by a brain tumor occurred when

Charles Whitman of Austin, Texas, took his guns up into the Texas Tower and used it as a gun platform to kill twelve people. He died with his guns.

Richard Speck, on the other hand, lived to go to prison after killing eight nurses in one long night of hell. He had suffered numerous head injuries as a child, augmented by episodes of heavy drinking and drugs. There is some evidence that he killed on other occasions, too, and so should be in the section on serial killers; however, that additional guilt has never been determined.

▌▌

A "Victim of Many Unusual and Irrational Thoughts"
Charles Whitman

I hate my father with a mortal passion.
And I can't stand the pressures on me.
I'm going to fight it out alone.

Charles Whitman in his final note

The pressures were definitely getting to him. The perfectionist personality that his father's demands had developed within him was finding it difficult to deal with the combination of maintaining a B+ average in his senior year in a field in which he did not want to practice ... coping with his mother leaving his wife-beating father ... part-time jobs to make financial ends meet ... obtaining his real-estate brokerage license. Those pressures eventually took him to the top of a twenty-eight-story tower in Austin, Texas, from which he killed twelve people.

Or did they? Perhaps those pressures could have been

withstood if "All-American Boy" Charles Whitman had not suffered from the additional pressure of a tumor growing on his brain.

"It's true, I was strict. With all three of my sons, it was 'yes, sir' and 'no, sir.' They minded me." Charlie Whitman was one of three sons born to Charles A. Whitman, a plumbing contractor in Lake Worth, Florida, and his wife. Young Charlie, the oldest son, learned early that it was safer to do exactly what his strict father demanded, otherwise a beating might come down on his head—or his mother's. He learned that any boy worth his salt had to know and be good with guns. "My boys knew all about [guns]. I believe in that," his father would later say.

Charlie learned, too, that he was expected to do the very best possible in anything he tackled. Charlie became an Eagle Scout at only twelve years old, a feat unusual in itself, but at the same time he was running the biggest and most efficient newspaper route in town and, of course, going to school. He became an adept pianist, one whom other parents held up as an example to their own children. People marveled at the good-looking, reliable, talented altar boy. No one knew, though, that he lived in terror of the possibility of his father beating his mother. No one paid any attention to the fact that he bit his nails constantly, because within his soul he knew that nothing he did could ever be good enough.

On graduating from high school in 1959, Charlie Whitman decided to join the Marines in order to capitalize on his love for and knowledge of guns, as well as to get away from his father in a manner that the father, whom he had come to hate and fear, could approve of. Charlie, who readily became a sharpshooter, served for a while at Guantánamo Bay, Cuba. When he discovered that the military would send him through school, he obtained an ROTC scholarship and went to the University of Texas to study engineering.

In 1962, he met and married Kathleen Leissner of Needville, Texas. The former "Queen of the Fair," who was studying to be a teacher, probably thought she was marrying a man who was as charming, strong, hardworking, and lovable as Charlie appeared on the surface to be. But what she got was a man who took out on her the hostility that sometimes accumulated and overcame him. She got a man who was into gambling to such an extent that he was charged in a military court-martial with gambling and loan-sharking, as well as with possession of an unauthorized pistol. As a result of that trial, he was demoted.

When Charlie failed to get as good grades in college as he needed to maintain his scholarship, he was forced to drop out of school, leave his wife, and return to finish his military enlistment. On its completion at the end of 1964, however, he returned to Austin, Texas, switched to architectural engineering, and determined to do better. This time his self-discipline let him do better. He carried an extra-heavy load of classes to make up for lost time, but he also decided that, though he was going to finish his degree, he didn't really want to be an architectural engineer. So while doing everything else, he also began studying for the real-estate sales exam in secret. All that in addition to working part-time to contribute to Kathy's earnings as a teacher and to pay for the new car he insisted that he had to have. He also became a Boy Scout leader, fondly teaching his troop the discipline and skills that he had enjoyed as a boy. That particular task, however, soon became too much for him to handle as thoroughly as he wanted, and he dropped out of scouting.

Too Much, Too Much

In March 1966, the pressures began to peak for the young man. Perhaps the final trigger was the arrival in Austin of his mother, who had finally gathered the courage to leave his abusive father. Perhaps that allowed him finally to admit the deep-seated fear he had that he would be just like his father, that his monumental self-discipline might be all that held his own violence in check.

Deciding that the only way out of the pressures on him was to let go of everything, Charlie made a snap decision to quit school, quickly selling his books and engineering tools, and then to leave Kathy, regardless of the fact that he loved her. A professor and friend took alarm and found a partial scholarship for Whitman, and gave him a chance to get caught up in his courses. Kathy, bewildered at what was going on, persuaded Charles to go talk to the psychiatrist at the university health center.

Though Whitman did not tell the doctor about the frequent virulent headaches he had been having, he told enough about the rages he felt consume him periodically for Dr. Maurice Heatly to write in his report: "He readily admits having overwhelming periods of hostility."

Charlie described to him a recurring thought he had of "going up on the tower with a deer rifle and start shooting people." Because people frequently have such thoughts, and the twenty-eight-story University of Texas tower had been the focus of many people's expressions of hostility, Heatly did not pay a great deal of attention to the remark, though he was concerned that the young man was disturbed and asked him to come back the following week. Whitman never returned. Instead, as he wrote in one of his final notes, he decided to "fight it out alone."

His struggle lay unnoticed by his wife and friends as summer school got underway. But underneath the normal facade he projected, he was feeling increasing rage, impulses toward violence that he feared made him exactly like his father, and a growing certainty that life had nothing worthwhile to offer him.

On Sunday, July 31, 1966, something brought Charles Whitman to an inner decision, one that gave him a strange calm noticeable even to his friends.

Kathy, who was working a split shift for the telephone company, was on duty that evening, so the two of them went out to dinner first, agreeing that he would pick her up from work at 10:00 P.M. Home alone, Charlie sat down at his typewriter and wrote, "I don't quite know what is compelling me to type this note." He told of his increasing fears and rages over the past weeks, much of it directed at the man he hated "with a mortal passion"

—his father. He made a point of saying that he loved Kathy, despite the fact that he intended to kill her after he picked her up. "I don't want her to have to face the embarrassment that my actions will surely cause her."

Charlie's best friend and his wife dropped over while he was writing his "suicide" note. The visitors found Charlie strangely placid and spent two hours chatting. When they left, Whitman drove to the phone company to pick up Kathy. There is no record that she saw anything wrong, but sometime around midnight, Charlie stabbed his pretty wife with a knife, killing her instantly. The rage was not dissipated, however.

He drove to his mother's apartment with a gun hidden under his clothing and asked the porter to let him in, in order to get a prescription drug that he needed very badly. The amiable man let Whitman in. His mother must have woken up to find her large, handsome, and now unrecognizable son bending over her, knife in hand. Terrified and stunned by bewilderment, she tried to escape, but he slammed her hand in a door hard enough to crush the bones in her hand and her diamond ring. He stabbed the mother he professed to love so very much in the chest and then shot her through the back of the head.

We don't know whether he wrote the note he left by her body before he killed her or after, but in thoroughly self-disciplined, orderly printing, Whitman wrote, "I have just killed my mother. I am very upset over having done it. However, I feel that if there is a heaven she is definitely there now. If there's not a heaven, she is out of her pain and misery. I love my mother with all my heart.

The intense hatred I feel for my father is beyond all description." He attached a quite different note to the door of the apartment, saying that his mother was ill and would not be going to work that day.

Returning to the little house where his wife lay dead, Whitman added to the letter he had previously written: "3 a.m. Wife and mother dead." Then, during the remainder of the summer night, he gathered and prepared his weapons—three rifles, a revolver, two pistols, a machete, a knife, and six hundred rounds of ammunition— to which he would add, after the stores opened, a shotgun purchased on credit from Sears. At 7:15 he rented a strong dolly for carrying all his equipment. At home, he placed his weapons in a military footlocker and gathered up the Marine duffel bag in which he had put canned food, water, a clock, pink toilet paper, and, because he was always conscious of the heat, a spray can of deodorant. Then, putting workman's overalls over his jeans and shirt, he drove to the tower that is the focus of the University of Texas campus.

Death from the Tower

The warm sun was beating down on the campus at 10:30 that Monday morning. It would make the air inside the observation platform of the tower sticky hot. The receptionist on the ground floor observed a workman arrive with his equipment on a dolly. Assuming that he had been called for repairs, she said nothing as he boarded the elevator.

On the twenty-seventh floor, where the elevator stopped,

Whitman manhandled his heavy equipment up three short flights of stairs to the twenty-eighth-floor observation deck. There, the clerk who maintained the guest register, Edna Townsley, forty-seven, looked up questioningly, only to have Charles Whitman shoot her, then use his gun butt to strike at her head. He pulled her from her desk and stuffed her into the space behind a couch.

Having gone out onto the platform, he was unpacking his duffel bag and his footlocker when he heard sightseers coming up the stairs to join him. He grabbed a loaded weapon. And so the first strangers died—fifteen-year-old Mark Gabour and his aunt, Margaret Lamport. Mark's mother and brother were both critically wounded.

Now Charlie Whitman was where his increasing hostility and unreasoned rages had brought him—standing on a platform, more than three hundred feet above the university campus, from which he could sight on anyone who moved for hundreds of yards around.

The first movement to catch his eye was made by an eighteen-year-old, Pat Sonntag, and his girlfriend, Claudia Rutt. The Marine marksman killed the promising ballet dancer with his first shot. When Sonntag, wide-eyed, threw himself down beside her, he died from Whitman's next bullet.

Gradually, shot by shot of the more than one hundred rounds he fired, Whitman cleared the campus for three blocks around. One man standing three blocks away remained out in the open, certain that no bullet could reach him, but he died with a sudden wound to the chest. A young woman, eight months pregnant with her first child, was struck in the abdomen. The bullet killed her unborn baby, then another killed the young man who tried to shield her. No one was safe from the powerful semiautomatic rifle anywhere in a one-hundred-eighty-degree angle from the tower.

As soon as the first shots were felt down on the ground, the authorities began their struggle to stop the mayhem. One policeman who crept forward and hid behind the base of a statue, hoping to get the sniper within his sights, died before he could fire. Soon others began shooting from cover in every direction, hoping to hit Whitman as he took aim, but when he ducked down and fired through drainage holes, they were helpless. They sent up a small airplane, hoping to attack him from the air, but his accurate and powerful fire punctured the fuselage, forcing the pilot to sheer away.

The time was nearing 1:00 P.M., and Whitman had been taking potshots at anyone who moved for close to two hours, when the police got into position to attack. They took a chance of being fired on to run for the tower, then took the elevator up. Two of them, knowing that there was no other way, climbed the stairs to the platform and broke through the barricaded door. Then each went a separate direction so that Whitman could not fire on them both at once. Two more men crept in. They saw that the sniper's hands trembled as he brought up his rifle to fire, but then he fell in a blast of gunfire, having finally achieved what he had wanted all along.

Charles Whitman's wife and mother, plus twelve strangers, lay dead. Thirty-one others were wounded. Whitman himself was dead.

An autopsy was performed on Charles Whitman as a matter of course. Within his brain the pathologists found a nut-sized tumor. It is a simplistic answer to assume that the tumor caused all those deaths and misery, especially in view of Whitman's own anger-filled life. However, the growth may well have been causing the headaches that had so distracted Whitman for the past few months, contributing to the increased difficulties he had in living up to his own expectations of himself. In addition, the tumor may have applied pressure to that portion of the brain that controls aggressive impulses, finally sending him to the top of the tower on a hot August day.

Newsweek magazine, covering the story two weeks later, wrote that those people who did not believe that the tumor was responsible "spoke in hushed tones of the dark tides of blood and violence that flow deep in the minds of most men, and which may sometimes break through the psychic controls that dam them up, flooding the victim's world with such surrealistic horrors that he is driven to seek his own destruction in one final explosive orgasm of death and destruction."

12

"Born to Raise Hell"
Richard Speck

> I should of been shot
> the first time I hit my mother.
> 　　　　　Richard Speck to Dr. Marvin Ziporyn

Perhaps, deep in his subconscious, nineteen-year-old Richard Speck knew something about what the biologists might be thinking concerning aggression when the future mass murderer had the startling words BORN TO RAISE HELL tattooed on his arm. Perhaps he had the feeling that his own biochemistry and history of head injury warred against him, bound to win out over his alternative urge to be a gentle person. Perhaps the fact that he killed eight young women in one four-hour siege and never remembered a thing about it. . . .

Before he came to Chicago and killed eight student

nurses, before he became a seaman whose shore leaves were invariably spent drunk, even before he married and transferred his hatred of his wife to any woman who appealed to him sexually . . . even before all those things, Richard Franklin Speck was a young man in pain who continually did aggressive things for which he could give no reason. Speck was born in December 1941 in Kirkwood, Illinois. From birth he seemed to be vulnerable to injury, ones that would play a major role in his becoming a killer.

It began when he was only three months old and contracted pneumonia. The physician told his mother at the time that lack of oxygen may have caused some damage that probably would not be noticeable until he was grown. After that, it was physical blows that did the cumulative harm.

As a tiny child, Richie had a shotgun fall on his head, leaving him dizzy for several hours. At only five, while trying to be a carpenter, he hit himself on the head with a hammer and again had a dizzy spell afterward. The next blow knocked him out: at ten he fell from a tree and was unconscious for at least an hour. His personality changed after that, making him easily irritable and quick to enrage. He also stopped putting any effort into his school work. The next year, while running, he accidentally drove his head against a steel awning rod. At fourteen he fell from a tree again, knocking himself out, and soon thereafter he rode his bike into a parked car, again knocking himself out.

Richard Speck's father died when he was six, after

which his mother began to move him and his five sisters throughout the Midwest, until she married again. Richie and his stepfather hated each other from the word go, and he moved out into the work world as soon as he could.

At age twenty Speck married fifteen-year-old Shirley Malone. Although she bore his daughter, her infidelity soon turned her into the object of his special hatred. The man who needed to be able to put his women on a pedestal decided he had a whore for a wife.

Soon after, he was arrested in Dallas, Texas, for holding a knife blade to a woman's throat. He later claimed that he thought she was someone else—a prostitute who owed him money—but he went to jail for a year and a half. He then began to make his way north, working occasionally on boats. While working on a Lake Michigan ore boat, he suffered an attack of appendicitis and was flown to a hospital in Hancock, Michigan. On recovering, he signed on another ore boat but was let go when it reached Indiana Harbor, south of Chicago.

Speck was in Chicago in July 1966, hoping to get some help from his sister, who lived there, and trying to get a ship so he could get back to work. On the night of the thirteenth, the twenty-five-year-old Texan was hanging around the National Maritime Union hiring hall by Calumet Harbor, where sailors found out which ships might need crews. He had been promised a job on an ocean freighter for the following week, but for now he could only wait and try to survive on the few dollars he had. He took a room at the Shipyard Inn.

He spent that Wednesday evening drinking with some

other sailors in a bar. He was already quite drunk when one of them offered him a pop of some drugs. Speck was never particular about what he used, even though he knew drugs had a real bad effect on him. He injected what they gave him, felt the welcome buzz begin to consume him . . . and knew nothing more until the following day. He apparently never has remembered what he did that night, but he accepted the verdict of the courts: that he had spent the hours from eleven until three or four the next morning terrorizing and killing eight student nurses.

Mass Murder

The figure who was later identified as Richard Speck undid a window screen at the back of one of the three townhouses on East 100th Street rented by the South Chicago Community Hospital as residences for some of their nurses. Reaching in, he was able to unlock the back door and creep in. There was no one there to challenge him, so, finding no one downstairs, he went on upstairs. There he knocked on a bedroom door. The knock awoke twenty-three-year-old Corazon Amurao, a Filipino student nurse working in Chicago on an exchange program. It was only 11:00 P.M., but she had yielded to a tiring day and gone promptly to sleep in the second-floor bedroom she shared with two other nurses. Her roommates, Merlita Gargullo and Valentina Pasion, also from the Philippines, had stayed up a few minutes longer than Corazon but had also quickly gone to sleep.

When the knock came on the door, Zony Amurao,

sleepy and puzzled, went to the door and turned the key. Immediately there was a push on the door. It swung wide and she saw a tall, pock-marked, darkly dressed man brandishing a gun in one hand and a knife in the other. The other girls awoke to terror, and the man, who smelled strongly of liquor, ordered the three of them into the hall. He stopped them at the second bedroom on the front, where he woke more women and herded them all into the back bedroom. There he held a gun on the three Filipino women plus Nina Jo Schmale, Patricia Ann Matusek, and Pamela Lee Wilkening.

The man kept talking, assuring them that he was not going to hurt them. When one of them nervously asked what he wanted, the man replied, "I want money. I'm going to New Orleans."

Hoping that money would send him away, the girls quickly volunteered to get what cash they had in their purses. Apparently he seemed gentle and earnest, unlikely to hurt them, so none of the girls made an attempt to get away as he let them go to their purses one by one. They just got what cash they had and returned to the room. Adroitly keeping the girls under the gun, the man cut up bed sheets and tied the girls' hands and ankles.

It was about 11:30 when Gloria Jean Davy arrived at the townhouse. The new president of the Illinois Student Nurses Association, she had been out for the evening. The intruder took her into the bedroom where the others lay and tied her up, too.

More than an hour had passed. The girls' initial fear had subsided in the flow of gentle chatter from the man, although he continually displayed signs of tension, tapping his gun on the floor, peering nervously out the window, making quick, abrupt movements while fingering the long butcher knife he carried.

Because he kept mentioning going to New Orleans, they were hoping he might be going to leave them soon when he went over to twenty-year-old Pamela Wilkening. "I have always wanted to be a nurse. I never liked to see people suffer," she had written on her application to nursing school. The man untied Pamela's ankles, ordered her to stand up, and took her out through the door, which he closed.

The girls left behind lay silent. A few minutes later they heard a very slight scream, one that was little more than a brief sigh. Pamela would later be found to have been stabbed in the left breast and strangled.

There had been silence for only a few minutes when Suzanne Bridget Farris, a Chicagoan, and Mary Ann Jordan, sister of Suzanne's fiancé, entered the house. Mary Ann was a student nurse, too, and had come to spend the night with her future sister-in-law, so that they could continue their discussion of plans for next spring's wedding. The pair climbed the stairs, chatting quietly, and walked into the back bedroom. Stunned, they discovered their housemates tied up. But they had no time to act; the man with the gun came up behind them and, instead of forcing them to lie down on the floor with the others, he directed them out of the room.

Corazon Amurao reported later that she heard them, too, make small sounds, halfway between gasps and screams, before she heard water running in the next-door bathroom. Suzanne Farris would be found in the bathroom, a mass of blood from eighteen stab wounds in her breasts and neck. She, too, had been strangled. Mary Ann Jordan, who would never be her sister-in-law, lay in the front bedroom, also violently stabbed. One of the stab wounds had penetrated her eye.

After the sounds of the intruder washing his hands in the bathroom, there was silence for about twenty minutes before he returned to the bedroom. That became a pattern throughout the horrible night. A friend of Amurao's dragged or carried from the room, sounds that she would not know until later meant death, the ritual cleaning up, then silence. No one knows what the man was doing during those long minutes before he returned to the bedroom to untie another victim.

The living girls left behind, finally realizing that something was horribly wrong, tried to scrooch under beds, hoping that they could avoid the killer's gaze. But on his return, he found them all, except for Corazon Amurao, who had rolled against the wall under the bunk bed. Perhaps because the killer knew there were eight women living in the house and he killed eight, he never realized that a ninth one was a visitor. One witness, Zony Amurao, was left alive, spending long hours in terror, lying motionless under the bed, wondering if he would find her.

Nina Jo Schmale, from west suburban Wheaton and queen of the spring dance, was next. She was strangled and stabbed in the neck four times. Her hands were still bound when she was found.

Again time passed, then he returned to take Valentina Pasion, who would get her wish to stay in the United States forever. Her bloody body was found in the second front bedroom by Nina's. She, too, had been stabbed in the neck.

This time, when the man returned, he carried Merlita Gargullo into the front room. The little Filipina who loved to dance was stabbed in the neck with a wound so deep that it severed her windpipe. Corazon reported hearing her murmur involuntarily the Tagalog word for "it hurts" before she, too, was strangled.

Patricia Matusek, who had that very day received word that she had been accepted to work after graduation at the prestigious Children's Memorial Hospital in Chicago, asked in fear-filled tones if the killer would untie her ankles so she could walk out of the room. She received a fierce kick to the stomach and was strangled.

Only Gloria Davy and Corazon Amurao remained now, but the latter was hidden. Her terror that she would be found only increased when the killer came for Gloria Davy. But this time he did not take his victim away. Through horrified eyes, Zony watched as the man removed Gloria's blue jeans. He unzipped his own pants and lay down on top of her. Corazon closed her eyes, but could not shut out the sounds of bedsprings squeaking rhythmically nor the rapist's polite voice asking, "Will you please put your legs around my back?"

The sounds continued for some minutes more, and

then there was silence again. It was several more minutes before Corazon realized that the pair had left the room. It would be hours before Gloria Davy's naked body would be found downstairs in the living room. During the forty-five or so minutes before the killer returned to the upstairs bedroom, Gloria would go through the hell of being raped and sodomized and having her rectum mutilated. She died of strangulation.

Later opinion would say that Gloria Davy had the horrible misfortune superficially to resemble Richard Speck's ex-wife, whom he hated with an abiding passion. She was the only one raped and the only one mutilated. There was some speculation that, in fact, he had intended only robbery until Gloria returned to the house and her resemblance to Shirley sent him into the frenzy of killing.

The killer returned to the bedroom where Corazon lay hidden, apparently to check if there was anyone left. Failing to see the tiny Filipina under the bed, he left the room. Corazon continued to cower against the wall, terrified that he had not left the house, until an hour or more after the girls' alarm clocks began to sound at 5:00 A.M. At last gaining the courage to move, she struggled against her bonds and was able to get them off. Relief turned to renewed horror when she ventured into the hallway and the front bedrooms. The stench of blood and the sight of her friends lying dead drove her out the front screened window onto a ledge at the front of the house. There she screamed, "All my friends are dead! Oh, God! I'm the only one alive!"

* * *

Analysis of a Killer

Some hours later, Richard Speck, who would never go to sea again, awoke in his room at the Shipyard Inn. By his side was a gun that he claimed he had never seen before (though he would later remember taking it from a whore the night of the murders). Puzzled, he washed up and discovered when he rinsed his hands that the water had turned red, as if his hands had been bleeding. That, too, puzzled him, but he forgot about it as he began to make the rounds of the neighborhood bars that afternoon. Among the leisured drinkers he met, news of the murders was beginning to circulate. When Speck realized that question-asking police were frequenting the same bars in which he hung out, he began to worry about the fact that he had run away from a burglary charge in Texas. He decided that he had better hightail it up to the North Side of the city.

In the meantime, the police had found a number of fingerprints inside the nurses' townhouse. Included in Amurao's description of the killer had been the very distinctive tattoo, among many on his arms, that said BORN TO RAISE HELL. The fact that the girls' wrists had been tied together with a sailor's square knot sent the police to the nearby maritime union hall. A clerk clearly remembered that tattoo and was able to locate the work application that gave Richard Speck's name.

On the Near North Side, Speck picked up a prostitute, paying her thirty dollars, more than he had had the night of the murder. When he hired another one, he found himself impotent, and they began to argue about money.

The woman called the police and reported that she had been with a client who had a gun. They came and took away the gun he was carrying since he didn't have a licence for it, but Speck's name had not yet been broadcast.

The next day, the police likeness derived from Corazon Amurao's description was published, but when Speck saw it, he failed to recognize himself. It wasn't until Saturday that he heard his name given on a news report, saying that Richard Speck was wanted for the murder of eight nurses.

That night, Speck registered in a flophouse under the name of Brian and tried to commit suicide by slashing his wrists. When he failed to die as quickly as he hoped, he called for help and was taken to Cook County Hospital. There an alert doctor saw the now-famous tattoo and remembered reading about it in that evening's newspaper. The police came quickly.

In Cook County Jail awaiting trial, Speck became friendly and talkative with the prison psychiatrist, Dr. Marvin Ziporyn. Ziporyn related in his book *Speck: The Untold Story of a Mass Murderer* the details of their conversations over the next few months. Ziporyn became convinced that Speck was telling the truth when he said that he had blacked out and could not remember the long hours during which he had, at a leisurely pace, killed the eight student nurses.

Although both Ziporyn and the other official court psychiatrists found Richard Speck competent to stand trial, Ziporyn alone became convinced that Speck's apparent psychopathic problems derived primarily from the numerous head injuries he had suffered as a child and teenager. Though the brain damage alone might not have sufficed to turn him into a killer, any inhibitions against criminality he might have had were erased by the combination of alcohol and drugs he had consumed that night.

Ziporyn gradually learned that Speck's family had known from his early childhood that he was possessed of two quite distinct personalities: one gentle, thoughtful, and respectful; and the other enraged and likely to strike out. That latter Richard appeared when he had been drinking or taking drugs, both of which he did regularly after about the age of twelve, though frequently just to relieve the vicious headaches to which he was subject.

The psychiatrist reported to Speck's attorney: "In brain damage, the problem is conduct disorder. Patients express deep remorse and retain the capacity for criticism of their own behavior, a self-criticism that seems to have a compulsive quality. There is often a big discrepancy between intellectual grasp and primitive behavior. As the psychoanalyst Dr. A. A. Brill said, these people are 'masters of what they saw, but slaves of what they do.' " They are prone to headaches, memory loss, and attacks of rage and aggression. "And most important—they have a reduced tolerance for alcohol and drugs. These things make them explode."

One psychiatrist discovered that Speck had a decidedly dual view of women, which Ziporyn identified as a madonna–prostitute complex. "His affable nature when sober invited sympathetic treatment by women, which he found unbearable because it seemed to sap his masculinity," said Ziporyn of one doctor's view, continuing: "He speculated that Speck's violence was triggered by a show of friendship by the nurses when they were touched by his gentle manner—something Corazon Amurao emphasized in her statement to police. This friendliness was another assault on his masculinity and moved him to violence."

"I've had lots of pleasure from women," Speck told Ziporyn. "I like them. All except one. I've got hate, jealous hate for her. Shirley. She's the only woman I've ever hit sober. Oh, yeah, and her mother." And that was another key point. As the psychiatrist told defense counsel: "It's a combination. Speck's personality, the brain damage, his bad experiences with his wife and the resultant hostility, the drugs, and the trigger of the chance resemblance of one of the girls to his wife—they're all vital components. Leave one out, any one of them, and you'd have had no crime."

Richard Speck was tried in Peoria, Illinois, about a hundred and fifty miles from Chicago, after his attorneys asked for a change of venue, figuring that he could not get a fair trial in Chicago. Instead of all the medical opinion the attorneys had, they used as his defense the assertion that he had been somewhere else at the time of the murders. A bartender from a saloon a mile and a half from the nurses' residence testified that Speck had been in Key's Pilot House bar and grill, eating a hamburger at midnight, when the killer was already inside the house and tying up the nurses.

But the jury paid little attention to the testimony of the

bartender and his wife. They remembered the sight of tiny Corazon Amurao stepping down from the witness stand, bravely walking toward Richard Speck, and exclaiming in her soft Filipino accent, "This is the man!"

After only forty-nine minutes of deliberation, they found Speck guilty of eight counts of first-degree murder. He was sentenced to die in the electric chair.

Soon after the trial, before the appeals had even begun to run their course, a factor was brought before the public that appeared, at first, to account for Speck's murderous personality. A study in Great Britain revealed that apparently a higher percentage of men in institutions (insane asylums, prisons, and homes for the retarded) had XYY chromosomes than was found in the general public. Normally, when a human egg is fertilized, it consists of either two X chromosomes—making a female—or an X and a Y chromosome—making a male. Sometimes, however, purely by accident, some males, often referred to as "supermales," receive an extra Y chromosome. Many biologists leaped on the idea that XYY men had an extra dose of aggression in them, aggression that could not be accounted for by psychological development. It was also pointed out that XYYs tended to be extra tall (Speck was six feet tall) and to suffer from acne (Speck's face had been scarred by acne).

Prominent in the information being spread at the time was the fact that the genetic makeup of a killer was used in two cases. In one, in Australia, twenty-one-year-old

Edward Hannell, who had stabbed an elderly widow to death, was found not guilty by reason of insanity, based on the fact that he was retarded and had the XYY chromosomes and thus "did not know that what he was doing was wrong." Some months later, in Paris, attorneys for Daniel Hugon tried the same defense against the charge of strangling a sixty-one-year-old prostitute. This time, however, the jury did not go along with the defense and Hugon was sent to prison for seven years.

It was widely anticipated that Speck's attorneys would use the XYY abnormality in an appeal of his death sentence, and numerous writers explained the genetic problem for the lay public, speculating on various ways the courts could decide. However, it turned out that Speck did not suffer that particular genetic malady. Gradually, such a defense idea was dropped as more and more scientists began to complete research that showed that the population in institutions had no higher incidence of the XYY chromosomes than did the general population outside the institutions. In addition, psychologists began to see that if the presence of the XYY chromosome did tend to make for an aggressive personality, it was probably only because XYYs tended to be taller than other people, and our society expects a more aggressive personality in a bigger person than it does from someone of average or short stature.

Although no additional charges were ever made, there was also considerable speculation over the fact that where Richard Speck had gone in the months preceding the Chicago murders, women had tended to disappear or turn up murdered. After being released from jail in Dallas, he had gone to Monmouth, Illinois, where he had spent part of his growing-up years. There he frequented a bar where the bar girl, Mary Pierce, whom he had tried to date, disappeared. Her body was later found in a pigsty near the tavern.

While he was recovering from having his appendix out in Hancock, Michigan, he began to date one of the nurses, who later reported that she found him to be a gentle man, but one apparently filled with hate, particularly toward his ex-wife. She did not regret it when Speck moved on toward Chicago. After he was turned off his ship at Indiana Harbor, three girls vanished from the nearby Indiana Dunes; they were never found.

Speck's death sentence was changed to life in prison after the U.S. Supreme Court decided that the death sentence was unconstitutional. He has applied for parole several times but has regularly been turned down.

PART VI

THE CHARISMATIC SERIAL KILLERS

A new word has entered the American vocabulary: *multicide*, the murder of many by one person. Even more recently, a consensus has been reached that the murder of many at approximately the same time, or in one "spree," is *mass murder*. In this book, Charles Starkweather, Jack Graham, Ronald DeFeo, Richard Speck, and Charles Whitman are regarded as mass murderers. In general, mass murderers are those killers who have reached a limit of some sort, perhaps the limit of the frustration they can bear, and decide to "speak their piece" in a glorious blaze, usually of gunfire.

Then there is the second category of multicide, the insidious horror of *serial murder*. In the main, the serial killer picks individuals that fit a certain category, most often women or young boys, and, one by one, visits them with horror and death.

Our perception of serial murder is that it is a new phenomenon in the life of America. However, the Federal Bureau of Investigation suspects that there might be as many as *five hundred* serial killers carrying out their horrible calling at any one time. If that is the case, it seems unlikely that serial murder could be something new. Instead, what is new is the ability of police forces all over the country to make connections among murder cases in different jurisdictions.

The mass killer murders in a short burst of overwhelming emotion. The serial killer controls the emotions enough to use his intellect both to avoid getting caught and to heighten the pleasure derived from killing. Going back in history, we find women who have been serial killers, especially of a sequence of husbands or children, and most often to collect the insurance money on their lives. The contemporary horror brought about by the serial killer, however, is that the victims can be anyone at any time or place, with no known relationship to the killer.

John Wayne Gacy of Chicago and Dean Allen Corll of Texas homosexually brutalized, tortured, and killed young men before being caught. Raymond Fernandez and Henri Landru attached themselves to lonely women, killed them, and moved on.

Three serial killers are covered in the following pages— Albert DeSalvo, the "Boston Strangler"; Kenneth Bianchi, who with his partner and cousin formed the murderous team known as the "Hillside Stranglers"; and, finally, Theodore Bundy, who needed no nickname to become known to the public. Each of these three possessed the apparent self-confidence, charm, and reasonably good looks to make them acceptable, even attractive, to women. And they used their appeal to select a target, get close to her, rape, bludgeon, or strangle her, and then move on . . . again and again. They were addicted to their crimes, and, like drug addicts, they were eventually overwhelmed and destroyed by their addiction. They let down their intellectual guard, and they were caught.

In *Serial Killers: The Growing Menace*, author Joel Norris enumerates twenty-one behavior patterns of people caught in the episodic violence that is typical of the serial killer. Each of the categories dealt with in this book (except demons, which is open to interpretation) is included, along with numerous others, from purely physical head injuries to knowledge from the earliest childhood that the killer was unwanted by his mother.

13

Strangler and Sex Addict
Albert DeSalvo

The feeling after I got out of that apartment
was as if it never happened.

Albert DeSalvo

First his mother turned her back on him by failing to
rescue him from the horrors inflicted on him by his
father. Then his wife, in whom he invested all his sexual
dreams, said, "Al, learn to control yourself!" and turned
her back on him, too. Finally, Albert DeSalvo killed
thirteen women when they turned their backs on him, but
he never paid for those murders.

A child of the Chelsea, Massachusetts, slums, born in
1931, the third of six children, Albert Henry DeSalvo
spent his childhood years in the sway of a violent drunk
of a father who laughingly paraded a perpetual chain of

prostitutes before his totally cowed wife and children. Once Frank DeSalvo forced the children to watch as he first beat his wife, knocking out all her teeth, and then broke each of her fingers, one by one, showing sadistic pleasure in the process. Al watched, too—at first reluctantly, later with wide-eyed panting—as his father demonstrated his sexual prowess. Apparently he began to try the sex act himself when he was no more than six or seven, and by eight he and his friends were forcing girls at school to perform ''blow jobs'' on them, enjoying the feeling of conquest, one he would savor all his life. His father showed him something else, too—how to shoplift from the stores in the neighborhood.

There was nothing about his mother that might have offset his father's influence. Instead, she was indifferent to the children, paying no attention to either their pleasures or their pains. She did nothing to change things when Al and his brother Joseph began to stay away from home each evening so that they would not be there when their father wanted to beat them, which he did every evening when he came home from his plumbing job. Five times over the years, Frank DeSalvo was arrested for assaulting his wife, too.

According to one report, the senior DeSalvo, probably when he was broke, ''sold'' Albert and two sisters to a farmer to work as ''slaves'' for a grand total of nine dollars. They were with the man for about six months, forced to do whatever he wanted them to, before Mrs. DeSalvo located them. When Al was thirteen, his mother finally divorced his father. She remarried a year later.

Even as a child, Albert began to practice the sadism that he himself experienced. He and a friend, whom he once came close to strangling, deliberately set neighborhood cats and dogs to killing each other. He and his friend also began to steal when the opportunity arose. As a teenager he developed a record for breaking and entering, though none of his arrests had to do with sex.

He grew to be an attractive young man whose "pretty boy" cuteness was offset by a large, hooked nose. He was proud of his dark, wavy hair, which he kept neatly combed. He was obsessed with sex, an attitude that at least one older woman found delightful when she took him in hand, at age fifteen, and taught him all the perversions she could.

At seventeen, after only one year of high school, Albert DeSalvo joined the army, staying in for eight years. Just as he had done at school, he became a favorite of those in authority, being eager to please. He served five of his eight years in Germany, where he became the army boxing champion and, off-duty, the army's sex champion, by taking every advantage of his appearance and knowledge to become a readily available partner for every lonely American wife whose husband failed to come home. Then, seeking love, not just sex, he met and married a German woman named Irmgard and brought her to the United States. Irmgard was from a highly respectable, middle-class family, and DeSalvo was certain that he was moving up in the world by marrying her.

From the day he met her, DeSalvo focused all his sexual interest on Irmgard, but his demands on her were many: intercourse five and six times a day, plus sexual activities so unusual that she began to find them repellent and created excuses not to give in to him so often. In addition, when she had her first baby, she found the process so painful that she feared getting pregnant again. And so another woman denied him the love he needed. He turned elsewhere for sex. When Irmgard discovered that, she rejected him even more coldly than before.

DeSalvo's less than legal sexual activity probably began while in Germany, but American police awareness of the adult, sexually addicted Albert DeSalvo began while he and Irmgard were at Fort Dix in New Jersey, perhaps after Irmgard had begun to reject him. At that time, in 1955, he sexually abused a nine-year-old girl. Her mother refused to press charges, and the army failed to prosecute, but DeSalvo's record had started.

Also while at Fort Dix, DeSalvo's daughter Judy was born. She was born with malformed legs which, the doctors said, would probably keep her from walking forever. Irmgard's rejection of Al strengthened with the fear that if she got pregnant again, she would produce another defective baby.

The couple moved to Malden, Massachusetts, and DeSalvo set about trying to be a good family man . . . but the terrible sexual need remained with him.

The following year, Irmgard and Albert returned to Germany to visit her parents. She was rejecting her husband's advances completely by that time, and so he pursued other women by using a routine of pretending to represent a beauty contest. He talked his way into feeling and measuring the beautiful girls he met, and many he was able to talk into much, much more. Al was quite adept at his persuasive con routine by the time he became known as the "Measuring Man" in Boston.

When Judy was two years old, her legs were put into a removable cast called a "frog cast" because of the position it held the legs in. Her parents were required to take it off four times a day to massage her upper thighs. Albert, proud of his strong hands, wanted to do the task as often as he could. The baby cried and, of course, he could not make her understand that the pain was necessary. When he finished the task and put the cast back on, he tied it with a special bow that he thought looked cute and girlish. The knot he used and the bow he tied were the same ones the Boston Strangler would later use in killing his victims.

"There was no more for me," he later said of this period. "It was always Judy, always Judy." Irmgard had nothing to give him.

Sometime in 1960, the very presentable—and clever—Albert DeSalvo developed a new scheme that would acquire for him all—or almost all—the sexual activity he could handle. He began to hang around the Harvard Square area, learning where attractive young women lived. Selecting one, he would follow her home and knock on the door. Then, utilizing the gift of persuasive gab at which he was particularly adept, he would persuade her that he represented a modeling agency and that her name had been given him as a prime candidate to be a model. He spent long minutes ostensibly checking out all her measurements, feeling her legs and breasts as he measured. He made sure that she understood that his opinion of her potential would be important to her future. As he left, he promised the excited girl that someone would be calling her soon. But, of course, no one did, and she would gradually realize she had been had. The man who had only one year of high school took great pride in having hoaxed the sophisticated college girls. He would later claim that he had sex with most of these young women. Only rarely did they contact the authorities about their strange, disappointing experiences.

The police regarded the mysterious "Measuring Man" as more of a pathetic nuisance than a danger. Gradually, however, twenty-nine-year-old DeSalvo began to do things that made him seem more dangerous, particularly breaking into apartments instead of being invited. In March 1961, DeSalvo was caught. As the story of his activities during the last couple of years came out, he bragged about his ability to sweet-talk well-educated women into doing what he wanted. Two months later he was sentenced to two years in jail for breaking and entering, but both the judge and a parole board believed his protestations that he would change his life, so he actually served only eleven months. He was released in April 1962. But he was released to a wife who put him "on probation." She called him an "animal" and insisted that he prove himself fit to be her husband again before she would engage in sex with him.

During the next few weeks, he regained a driver's license, though it permitted him to drive only during daylight hours, and he took a job with a construction firm that sent him all over the Boston area checking into the functioning of various diesel engines used on job sites. During the day, there was no one who was required to check into the whereabouts of sex-maniac Albert DeSalvo.

Death and Sex

Flag Day, June 14, 1962, was followed by eighteen months of killing, thirteen victims, and eighteen months of building hysteria, during which one killer kept the Boston area gripped in fear.

It was a Thursday, the not-very-noticeable holiday called Flag Day, in Boston, Massachusetts. DeSalvo lied to Irmgard about going fishing and instead roamed around Boston looking for an appropriate apartment for one of his scams. When he rang the doorbell of Anna Slesers, a fifty-five-year-old Latvian-immigrant seamstress, he was carrying the lead weight off his lobster net. Anna was bathing and dressing in preparation for spending the evening at a service commemorating the date when the Soviets shipped thousands of Latvian citizens to Siberia. Her son was to pick her up at her small apartment and take her to the service. When the doorbell rang, she answered it in her bathrobe. The dark-haired man standing there brashly entered the apartment, claiming that he had been sent to do some work. When she turned her back on him to go into the kitchen, he quickly hit the woman on the head with the lead weight. She fell on top of him, knocking him down. The blood from her head wound gushed over him and he suddenly felt a need to strangle her. Pulling the belt from her robe, he wrapped it around her neck and carried out his grotesque sexual activities.

Leaving the apartment, he felt that someone else had carried out the murder and molestation, a feeling of apartness that Albert DeSalvo would experience after each murder.

When Anna Slesers's son called for her, he received no answer to his loud knocks. Breaking in the door, he found his mother dead. At first it looked as if she had hanged herself with the cord of her bathrobe, but then the authorities realized that the cord had to have been used by someone else to strangle the gray-haired woman. With her robe pushed completely open and her bent legs spread grossly apart, she no longer looked like someone's beloved mother. She had been molested but not raped. Her apartment had been ransacked, but there was no sign that anything was missing. The cord that strangled her was arranged so that its ends made a slight bow.

Years later, to psychiatrist James A. Brussel, DeSalvo speculated, ''Maybe in my own mind I falsely thought'' that sex with Irmgard would improve after that. But it didn't.

Less than two weeks later, probably June 25, Mary Mullen, eighty-five, opened the door to a man who said that he had come to do some work on her apartment. When he put his hands around her neck, she had a heart attack and died instantly. Mary's death would not be known as the work of the Boston Strangler until he confessed it many months later.

June 30, a Saturday morning, some miles north of Boston, in Lynn. Sixty-five-year-old Helen Blake was going about her usual early morning weekend chores when her doorbell rang. Sometime soon after that she died, face down on her bed, strangled by a nylon stocking. Neighbors began to worry about her on Monday, and she was found that evening. Her legs were spread wide—in the "frog cast" position, with her pajama tops pushed up around her shoulders. Her bra had been tied under the deadly stocking so that its straps made the shape of a bow. She had been attacked but not raped, though many parts of her body had been bitten. DeSalvo had killed the somewhat overweight woman in the kitchen—where he had politely handed her the milk bottles he had found beside the front door—and then carried her into the bedroom, where her body was arranged on the bed. Her apartment was strewn with the contents of pulled-out drawers and broken chests, though apparently nothing was missing.

DeSalvo spent the next few hours just riding around Boston, enjoying the summer day. Then he got the urge again and rang the bell of alert and active sixty-eight-year-old Nina Nichols. She was on the telephone with her sister at five o'clock discussing their plans for dinner that evening when she hung up to answer her buzzer. She never showed up for dinner. The gray-haired, semiretired physiotherapist was found dead in her destructively ransacked apartment several hours later. She had been strangled with two nylon stockings, the ends of which were arranged in curves, as if representing the loops of a bow. Her slip was pulled up around her waist and her legs were spread wide. Mrs. Nichols, too, had been molested but not raped, although the mouth of a wine bottle was pushed into her vagina.

Years later, in his confessions, DeSalvo would claim that he made no preparations in advance. He did not study a woman and wait until the time was right. He just walked into whatever building he could get into most easily, pressed a number of buttons, and went to the door that opened. He said that he could tell instantly what approach to take with the woman at the door. Then his gentle, believable face and manner took him into the apartment.

August 19, a Sunday, another hot day. Ida Irga, seventy-five, a long-time widow, died after telling her sister on the telephone that she would do some cooking for her. Two days later, her worried sister asked the building caretaker to enter the apartment. He sent his thirteen-year-old son, who was met by the horrific sight of the elderly woman lying on the floor, her legs spread wide and propped up on chairs. Mrs. Irga, too, had been strangled, this time by human hands, although a pillow case had been pulled tight around her neck.

Older women living alone were, by this time, completely panic-stricken at the thought of the man the papers were calling "The Sunset Killer." They were unaware that another of them was already lying dead in her apartment in Dorcester, across Boston from Ida Irga's apartment.

August 20, a Monday. Jane Sullivan, a sixty-seven-year-old nurse who worked the night shift, was home during the day, and she died during the day. Her body was found ten days later, propped in the bathtub, with face and arms under water, her buttocks obscenely in the air. She had been strangled by two stockings, and then her bulky body placed in the tub. Again, she had been attacked sexually but not raped. Again, her apartment had been searched.

In his confessions many months later, DeSalvo would be adamant that only once in all his intrusions into women's apartments had he ever stolen anything. That once was twenty dollars that he had found on a shelf in Anna Slesers's closet. However, he really had no answer as to why he had felt it necessary to thoroughly ransack the apartments of the women he killed.

Nor could he explain why he attacked older women. "When this certain feeling comes on me, it's a very immediate thing," he would say later. When he was ready, it didn't matter how old the woman might be.

For the next three and a half months Boston knew no more attacks, just continuing fear that the status could change at any moment. When it did, it changed dramatically and in such a way that all women lived in terror, not just older women.

December 5, a wet, cold Wednesday early afternoon, DeSalvo's wedding anniversary. A twenty-nine-year-old woman living in a Back Bay apartment answered her door soon after 2:00 P.M. to a smiling man murmuring something about painting to be done. He seemed friendly and personable, but then his conversational subject changed from the state of her ceiling to the shape of her body. She quickly and ingeniously lied about the presence of her husband in the next room. The man, who, she said, was between twenty and thirty, quickly left. But the need to give in to that "certain feeling" had not left DeSalvo.

Sophie Clark, a twenty-year-old black medical technology student, went home at lunchtime that day to the apartment she shared with two other girls in the building next to the ingenious liar. A roommate found her at 5:30. Sophie had been strangled with a cord made of three stockings twisted together. She had first been gagged. She lay on her back, her legs spread wide. Apparently she had put up a fight before dying. Medical investigators found that for the first time the killer had forced his penis into a victim's vagina and had an orgasm.

Because the killer had not just masturbated over his victim and the victim was young and black, many investigators thought that Sophie Clark had been killed by someone else, perhaps someone who had deliberately imitated the Boston Strangler.

December 29 or 30, an apartment also in Back Bay, where the single women who had, long before, been approached and raped by a friendly seeming dark-haired man had never passed on the word to the next tenants. Patricia Bissette, a twenty-three-year-old secretary, had done her laundry on Saturday as usual, then was not seen again until she was found on Monday morning. Early Sunday morning, DeSalvo entered her apartment by snicking back the lock with plastic and woke Pat Bissette from a sound sleep. Extraordinarily, she believed his lie about living in the building and having mutual friends. She rose and made coffee for the killer.

Unlike other victims of the Strangler, Patricia Bissette was not left naked and exposed. Instead, she was found lying on her bed, a cover drawn up under her chin. But beneath that cover she lay with her pajamas rucked up to her shoulders and with three stockings knotted together with a silk blouse to form a tight noose around her neck. Her room had been searched, as usual.

On February 18, 1963, DeSalvo again made an early morning call at an apartment. An attractive, twenty-nine-year-old German waitress answered. When "the repairman" tricked her into turning her back on him, he attacked as usual, but this woman fought him. She bit his hand and proceeded to kick and punch, all the time biting hard on his finger. When the shaken man finally got loose, he just grabbed his jacket and ran. To people responding to her screams, he cleverly held up his bleeding hand and shrieked something about having barely gotten away from the attacker. DeSalvo hurried to the old family attorney, who had obtained a divorce for his mother and defended him on the breaking-and-entering charges, in order deliberately to create an alibi. As far as is known, this woman is the only potential murder victim to have escaped the Strangler. Perhaps he failed to kill her because he did still love his German wife.

March 9, 1963, Saturday, in the old mill town of Lawrence. For some reason he never understood, DeSalvo, entering an apartment building, saw and picked up a short brass rod. "We got to paint the kitchen," he told sixty-nine-year-old Mary Brown when she answered the door. Then he struck her with the rod when she turned her back. He ripped open her clothing and continued to strike her, until her head was a pulpy mass. He contributed to the blood by stabbing her in the right breast with a fork. Before leaving, he found a white sheet on a chair and covered her body with it.

This killing would not be recognized as the work of the Strangler until he himself confessed to it. Thus it seemed to the public as if more than four months had passed between killings. But there were, in the intervals, other attacks that did not result in death. These would not become known until years later . . . if ever.

Monday, May 6, in Cambridge, across the Charles River from Boston, early in the morning. Beverly Samans, a twenty-three-year-old graduate student in counseling, was struggling with a desire to be an opera singer instead of a counselor, though she was slightly deaf. Barely awake and getting ready to go to class, she answered her door to a man who said he had come to paint. She grudgingly let him in, only to be faced by a knife and a demand for intercourse. He tied her hands behind her and put a small gag in her mouth, though she was able to talk—and scream—around it.

"She made me feel so unclean, the way she talked to me. . . . *'Don't do it, it's not nice'*—Irmgard said that to me just the night before," he later recalled. When her yells and complaints distracted him from playing with her, DeSalvo grabbed up another knife he had brought with him and began to stab her. Beverly Samans was found two days later with a cord of stockings and handkerchiefs around her neck, but she had not been strangled. She had died from twenty-two stab wounds.

The entire hot summer of 1963 passed before the Strangler struck again. During that time, some of the authorities became convinced that there were actually two Stranglers at work, one going after the older women and one after the young ones.

Erle Stanley Gardner, the creator of Perry Mason and the founder of the Court of Last Resort, wrote an article about the Boston Strangler in *The Atlantic Monthly* about this period, and he marveled that the Strangler was still finding it so easy to enter women's apartments: "Despite the warnings, despite all of the publicity in the press, despite the fact that many of the women who are living alone in Boston are now armed with tear-gas guns, safety devices on the doors, and a firm determination not to open the door to any stranger, the Strangler enters, perpetrates his crime, and vanishes."

September 8, a Sunday, in suburban Salem. Evelyn Corbin, a divorcée who was fifty-eight but appeared to be in her forties, had breakfast with a neighbor whose son she dated. Then she went to dress quickly before picking the friend up for church. In the half hour before she was expected, DeSalvo forced the attractive assembly-line worker to bring him to orgasm manually. For her pains, he strangled her with stockings. The neighbor found her, lying on her bed, fully exposed and savagely assaulted. Another stocking was tied in a neat bow on her ankle, which hung off the side of the bed. Her own underpants had been used to gag her.

November 23, the day after President John F. Kennedy was assassinated, early afternoon. As the rest of the world mourned in front of the television, the killer entered the Lawrence apartment of a twenty-three-year-old designer, Joann Graff, and raped and killed her, all within not much more than five minutes. She was found the next day lying on her bed, stocking-and-leotard noose tightened around her neck, the imprints of teeth on her left breast. Later, an upstairs neighbor would report that a man in his late twenties had knocked on the door opposite his; when the neighbor had asked who he wanted, the visitor had asked for Joann Graff, with the name pronounced wrongly.

On January 4, 1964, the final Strangler murder took place. The victim was Mary Sullivan, only nineteen and no relation to Jane Sullivan, killed sixteen months earlier. She had lived in the Beacon Hill apartment only four days, having excitedly moved into Boston from Hyannis. Everything about Mary's death was more than before. She had been strangled, yes, but it was done by hand. Yet *three* nooses were around her neck: a gray stocking covered by a pink silk scarf covered by a flowered scarf. And obscenely inserted into her vagina between her elevated and spread-apart legs was the handle of a long broom. A fluid that turned out to be seminal fluid was still dripping from her mouth when her roommates found her.

Psychiatrists at Work

Not long after Mary Sullivan's death the authorities brought in experts to develop a psychiatric analysis of the killer from the evidence shown by the murders themselves. The experts studied every discernible pattern as well as the differences among the killings. The preponderance of this committee favored the idea that more than one man had been at the lethal business. Psychic Peter Hurkos, brought in by private citizens, believed that it was only one man. And Dr. James A. Brussel, the psychiatrist who had analyzed the characteristics of the "Mad Bomber" of New York, firmly believed that the pattern among the details of the killings reflected changes going on in the mind of a single killer. He called the changes "instant maturity" and said, "In this two-year period, he has suddenly grown, psychosexually, from infancy to puberty to manhood." The murders were "the only way he knew to solve his problems, find himself sexually, and become a grown man among men."

Brussel thought that the early murders reflected a little boy's curiosity about—as well as anger at—his mother, leading to his poking and prodding at an older woman while unable to actually carry out intercourse. His sexual curiosity and his need to punish then transferred themselves from his mother to girls of his own age, with intercourse attempted but not fully achieved. The indignities he visited on them grew, until, finally, with the last one, Mary Sullivan, he achieved his mature goal. He, in effect, "cured himself" and thus probably would not kill again. His revenge against his wife was over.

Brussel also decided that the killer was probably in his late twenties or early thirties, muscular, highly sexed, of average height and appearance, clean, and well-spoken. Brussel even predicted that the killer would have well-maintained, attractive hair.

Albert DeSalvo, who would later be seen to possess all those predicted characteristics, forsook Massachusetts that summer and fall for nearby Connecticut. Week after week, as opportunity presented itself, he forced his way into women's apartments, tied them up, and treated them obscenely for long, horrible minutes. On one day he was known to have invaded the homes of four different women. However, none of the victims died; he now seemed to need his women awake and responding, instead of dead. He even sometimes released them and left if they cried a great deal. But in those months, over a hundred different women reported the episodes to the police. DeSalvo acquired a new nickname: "The Green Man," because he usually wore dark green work pants.

In October, DeSalvo took his insatiable activity back to Massachusetts. On the twenty-seventh, he entered the Cambridge apartment of a new bride. Hoping to save her life, she let herself be tied to the bed and forced into several long hours of obscenities with him. Oddly enough, he eventually murmured an apology to her and left. The quaking but living woman reported him to the police. Because of his history as the "Measuring Man," the police looked into DeSalvo's whereabouts. The twenty-year-old victim readily identified him. So too did a number of his Connecticut victims once the police had distributed his photograph. He was arrested again, and— he said later—because things had been going better for him (his wife was kinder; his boss liked him), he began to seek relief in confession. He was not yet being considered as a possible Boston Strangler.

When Irmgard came to see him in jail, the police learned—almost more by her evasions than by her statements—that Albert DeSalvo had an insatiable sex appetite. He readily admitted—even bragged a bit—to breaking into residences and forcing his vile attentions on women. After hearing from the police in four states, the prosecution estimated that he had molested at least four hundred women. DeSalvo was sent to Bridgewater State Hospital to be evaluated.

Found fit to stand trial, he began to act strangely enough that he was returned to Bridgewater again. There he became acquainted with another prisoner being investigated closely as a possible Boston Strangler. DeSalvo gradually said things that turned the officials' attention to him. The other prisoner's attorney was F. Lee Bailey, the trial attorney who had gained national fame for getting Cleveland osteopath Sam Shepherd out of prison after he had been convicted of killing his wife. As his client began to tell Bailey the tales DeSalvo had told him, Bailey started working with the police to discover if DeSalvo's claims could be true.

In early March, Bailey became DeSalvo's attorney and, oddly, set about proving that his new client was indeed the Boston Strangler. He was determined to set the mind of Boston at peace as well as to make sure that the man who had kept the city in fear for two years was incarcerated.

Bailey called in a specialist who hypnotized DeSalvo and got him to describe some of the scenes of the murders in the hope that he would give details that he could know only if he were indeed the killer. During that process, DeSalvo talked about massaging the women as if they were his daughter Judy, whose legs he had massaged for long hours, days, and weeks. All the women he attacked were his daughter Judy, whom he secretly wanted to strangle. They were also all his wife, Irmgard, whom he hated for rejecting him and who did not like having her neck touched. They were also all his mother, whom he loved but who had failed to protect him from his father.

After hearing DeSalvo's complete story, Bailey would later write, "DeSalvo was without doubt the victim of one of the most crushing sexual drives that psychiatric science has ever encountered."

The Boston police were gradually coming to realize that even if DeSalvo confessed, they would be unable to find sufficient evidence to actually *prove* in court that he was the Boston Strangler. They developed a plan by which, with all the legal safeguards necessary, DeSalvo could freely confess to the details of all the murders and none of it would be used in court against him. If it became quite clear that he was indeed the murderer and the psychiatrists found that he had been sane, the prosecutors were willing to prosecute him just on the "Green Man" attacks, knowing that those charges would be sufficient to keep him in prison for a long, long time. If he were found to have been insane, the actual court proof of guilt would not be required anyway.

And so Albert DeSalvo began his long confession sessions, during which he told the details of each of the thirteen murders committed by the Boston Strangler. The one thing he was firm about during the long months before his trial was that he wanted psychiatric treatment to help him understand why he did the horrible things he did. But that was not to be.

DeSalvo's trial was delayed again and again, mainly for political reasons. But he was finally brought to court for his "Green Man" activities on January 9, 1967, in Cambridge. The jury paid little attention to the psychiatric witnesses who insisted that DeSalvo was insane and had been under the influence of an "irresistible impulse" when he committed the Boston Strangler's thirteen murders of women who had turned their backs on him. The jury found him guilty and sentenced him to prison.

In February, before he was sent from Bridgewater State Hospital to prison, he and two other inmates escaped, sending Boston into a paroxysm of terror. However, he left a note saying he was leaving because he wanted psychiatric help and couldn't get it in prison. A day and a half later, DeSalvo gave himself up. He had had no desire to hurt anyone while he was outside, he just wanted help. Instead he was sent to Walpole State Prison where, in 1973, the Boston Strangler was stabbed to death by other inmates.

14

"You Can Call Me Steve"
Kenneth Bianchi, One of the Hillside Stranglers

I belong out. Ken belongs gone.
I belong out in the world where I can do
what I fuckin' want to!
           Steve, Ken Bianchi's alternate personality

Kenny Bianchi was one of a pair of men who raped, strangled, mutilated, and trashed young women in Los Angeles in the late 1970s. Kenny's partner in the serial murders was his cousin, Angelo Buono. Kenny was also one of another pair—he and Steve. But Steve was the one who gleefully participated in the LA killings and then went on to—less adeptly—kill two girls in Bellingham, Washington. But both members of this pair were within the single body of Ken Bianchi. Or—was there, finally, just one Ken Bianchi, a young, conscienceless killer with a facility for using whatever means came to hand to help himself out of a difficult situation?

(Note that in the following tale the emphasis is on Ken Bianchi, though he was only one of the pair of Hillside Stranglers. His cousin, Angelo Buono, never talked. In addition, it is probable that Bianchi started murdering before he joined forces with Angelo, just as he went on killing after they parted company.)

Nicholas Bianchi and Frances Buono both came from large families—thirteen brothers and sisters between them—so when it turned out that they could not have their own children, they were in despair . . . until they were able to adopt a baby boy whom they called Kenny. They thought they were getting a perfect treasure. They didn't know of the harm that may already have been done to him, harm that they would only make worse as he grew.

Kenny was the illegitimate son of a promiscuous, probably alcoholic fourteen-year-old who was mortified by what an unwanted pregnancy was doing to her life. Feeling no temptation to hold her son when he was born, she promptly gave him away to an uncaring foster mother who regularly tried to pawn him off on neighbors rather than care for him herself. Those neighbors who were willing to take him for a day or so generally ignored him, and probably never even noticed when he had been moved on to another foster mother. During the first weeks of his life, he had none of the loving holding and touching that a newborn needs to experience in order to learn to relate to other people.

The Bianchis of Rochester, New York, arranged privately to adopt the three-month-old boy no one wanted, and in

1952 he became legally theirs. But that fact did not allow them to relax. Frances, in particular, found daily reasons to fear that he might be taken away from them, through disease or accident. Passing on her own tendency to hypochondria, the nervous woman regularly saw physical ailments in Kenny that sent her anxiously scurrying to the doctor with him. Afraid of accidents, she refused to allow him to play with friends on the playground. He rapidly became a two-sided individual: sweet and fun to others, but a behavioral stinker—subject to profound temper tantrums—the moment his adoptive mother came in sight. He also became a perpetual liar, adept at telling others what he thought they wanted to hear—or what would keep him out of trouble.

Unfortunately, Kenny suffered from a urination problem that made him wet his pants many times during the day and night. Mrs. Bianchi's love and understanding quickly became abuse as she tried punishment as a cure for the situation. Seeking a medical solution, she took him to doctor after doctor, forcing on Kenny the pain and indignity of genital examinations. Years later, psychiatrists would say that he probably felt those exams as sexual abuse. He frequently missed school because of his urination problem and at one time was kept home for several months. Ken may not have minded that, however, because the other children were unmerciful in their teasing. In addition, reports were often sent home from school accusing Kenny of various misbehaviors that the boy, appearing bewildered, swore positively that he had never done.

Tensions in the household became even worse when Kenny was eight, after Mrs. Bianchi persuaded the easygoing Nicholas, a foundry worker, to buy a house they could not afford. Meeting the mortgage payment became a monthly crisis for the whole family. One report for the Rochester Society for the Prevention of Cruelty to Children, which author Ted Schwarz quoted in *The Hillside Strangler: A Murderer's Mind*, revealed that the social worker "found mother to be a deeply disturbed person, socially ambitious, dissatisfied, unsure, opinionated, and overly protective."

On one occasion when his domineering mother hit Kenny, he ran up to his room and hid under his bed. There, instead of being alone, he discovered a sympathetic friend from within himself, a self-confident boy named Steve. Steve was very angry over the way Kenny was being treated, and he encouraged Kenny to run away and even to hit his mother back when she struck him. Steve stayed around for quite a while, doing the things that Kenny would like to have done but didn't have the nerve to do. However, as Kenny grew, Steve didn't come to see him so often. He gradually disappeared from Ken's awareness. Instead, Steve would do things that got Ken into trouble, but Ken wouldn't know how the things had happened. It would not be until many years had passed and Ken Bianchi was in prison awaiting trial for the murder of two Bellingham, Washington, girls that psychiatrists would expose the rage-filled Steve and bring him to Ken's awareness again.

Within only a couple of years, Nicholas Bianchi failed

to keep up the payments on the wonderful house Mrs. Bianchi had insisted they have, and the mortgage was foreclosed. So not only was Frances a failure at having children, now she had also failed at keeping a home. Mr. Bianchi became happier with the financial pressure relieved, but Mrs. Bianchi could not accept the fact that she had to go out and work, although her absence took considerable pressure off Ken.

Several times during his growing-up years, school officials requested that Kenny be looked at by psychologists because of his complete lack of attention to school work. Usually, when Kenny's problems were investigated, the psychologists recommended that Mrs. Bianchi, too, should have help for the benefit of the whole family, but she never acknowledged that anything might be wrong with her, and she refused to consider psychiatric help.

Always, Mrs. Bianchi placed the blame for any problems the family might have on someone else—the doctors, the schools, the social workers, the neighbors. Kenny learned well his lesson in offsetting the blame.

At thirteen, Kenny finally began to turn to his father for some companionship. But, one day at work, Nicholas Bianchi suffered a heart attack and died, leaving Ken to the unadulterated mercies of his thoroughly neurotic mother.

Kenny turned into a handsome, dark-haired teenager who attracted the girls by his courtly manners and their mothers by his clean-cut looks and exemplary behavior. At home, though, in the privacy of his own bedroom, he devoured sex magazines and whatever pornography he could find. He was most interested in what he saw of sexual violence.

Brenda Beck was a friend of Ken's own age, whom he had known since he was little. At age eighteen, in an attempt to break away from his mother, he married Brenda. However, he soon convinced himself that she had not been a virgin when he married her and that she was giving herself sexually to the men she worked with in her job as a nurse. He himself, living by a different standard, continued to see other girls. The marriage failed after only a few months.

Ken's major ambition was to become a policeman. He studied for the examinations but was rejected and turned to security work. In that position, he was able to indulge his natural inclination to take those objects that attracted him. He was never charged with theft, but he was required to change jobs often, resulting in him acquiring a bad reputation.

During those years of the early 1970s, three children died in Rochester in horrible circumstances. The first, a partially clothed ten-year-old Puerto Rican named Carmen Colon, was seen running from a car on November 16, 1971. No one stopped to help her, and her dead, battered body was found two days later. Eighteen months later, eleven-year-old Wanda Walkowicz died of strangulation after being raped. Her body was found on a hillside. Finally, in November 1973, another eleven-year-old, Michelle Maenza, was found in the same condition.

Because the three girls all had alliterative names, the

killings acquired the name "The Double Alphabet Murders." They were never solved. Years later it would become known that the car seen chasing Carmen Colon was identical to the one driven by young Kenneth Bianchi at that time. He was never a suspect until years later, even though in 1972 he wrote a letter to a girlfriend in which he rather proudly confessed that he was suspected. She never showed that letter to anyone, figuring that it was just another example of the fantasy life (also called lying) that Ken Bianchi engaged in.

California Life and Death

About the time of the last child murder, Bianchi began to find the thought of moving to California attractive, but it took him another two years to gather the courage to move away from his mother. His cousin, Angelo Buono, agreed that his younger cousin from the East could stay with him until he found a place to settle in Los Angeles.

Kenny discovered immediately that his cousin in Glendale, seventeen years older, led the kind of life that he wanted. Although the automobile reupholsterer was divorced and the father of eight children, he was the focus of a chain of teenage girls who found him to be their hearts' desire. They found his dark Italian virility fascinating and were willing to learn all he could teach them about sex. There were always girls around, and Angelo was willing to share them with the newcomer— whether they liked it or not. Another thing Kenny quickly learned was the effectiveness of Angelo's fake police badge. When he wanted to con a reluctant female into going with him or a prostitute into accepting the fact that he wasn't going to pay, he just flashed the badge.

Again Ken applied to be a policeman. He was rejected on the basis of his test scores, although his articulateness about his reasons for wanting to be a cop was impressive. Even so, he remained enthusiastic about police work and arranged to participate in a "ride-along" program that let interested civilians ride in patrol cars on duty.

After some months, Angelo, tired of having Ken around, ousted him from his house. Kenny finally got a job as a land-title researcher, bought himself a car—a very impressive Cadillac bought with down-payment money provided by his mother—and rented an apartment. He was all set for all the girls he wanted. Many of them fell in love with him, but, like Brenda, they quickly got fed up with his possessiveness.

At a company party to welcome in 1977, Ken Bianchi met Kelli Boyd. Soon they were living together and within weeks Kelli was pregnant. Despite his apparent devotion, Kelli did not rush to marry Ken because he was not as steady as she wanted in a husband. One excuse he gave for occasionally skipping work was that he was suffering from cancer and had to spend long sessions at the hospital receiving chemotherapy. The shocking thought that he might die of cancer kept her from asking too many intrusive questions when he was out in the evening. It also kept her from marrying him.

Looking for ways to earn more money, Ken and Angelo decided that they would set themselves up as pimps. They deliberately set out to entice Sabra, an attractive teenage would-be model, into becoming financially, and then emotionally, dependent on them and forcing her to work as a prostitute. They frequently beat her, and they kept all the money she earned, reinforcing her dependence.

One of the high school girls who hung around Angelo assumed that he was going to marry her. He forced her into having an abortion, she suffered a miscarriage, and still she gave in when he demanded that she participate in a lucrative orgy he wanted to set up with a group of men and Sabra. Most of the participants were officials in the governments of the various towns around Glendale. Satisfied with the evening, one of the men gave Ken a County of Los Angeles seal to put on his car. It really only entitled him to free parking, but he would later use it to enhance his authority when pretending to be a policeman with the girls he aimed to kill.

Sabra brought another girl into the business. When that girl went on a call to a client who happened to be a lawyer, she told him what was going on. He took her away from Angelo and Ken. Though the men threatened the lawyer, some goons brought in by the lawyer frightened Angelo into letting the matter drop.

"Some girls don't deserve to live!" the angry Angelo snarled. Ken (or Steve), always seeking the older man's approval, started to brood on that idea. Their urgency to do something to "show" the girls who might defy them doubled when Sabra managed to escape their supervision and disappear. They got a new girl to move into Angelo's house, but she only enraged him by refusing to let him sodomize her. Finally the two men stopped just talking about strangling a "cunt" and put a plan into action.

The Hillside Murders

In acquiring a list of possible clients for their operations, Angelo and Ken became acquainted with an attractive black prostitute named Yolanda Washington, who was raising a small son on her earnings from the street. When their anger at the girls who didn't "deserve to live" boiled over and they decided that it was time to kill one of them, they remembered Yolanda. They knew where the girl's turf was on Sunset Boulevard, and so, on the night of October 17, 1977, they went hunting her.

Ken and Angelo used their pretend-police tactics to get Yolanda into their car, where they handcuffed her. As Angelo drove, Ken/Steve forced the girl to disrobe and then raped her. As a horrible finale, he threw her legs over the back of the front seat, so that Angelo, driving with his left hand, could hold her down with his right arm while Ken strangled her. Then they got off the freeway and discarded the naked, dead girl on a slope near the entrance to Forest Lawn Cemetery.

Then Ken returned to Kelli. He was finding her pregnancy fascinating. She wasn't so sure.

Halloween night, Hollywood Boulevard. Judy Miller, fifteen, one of the thousands of hopeful youngsters who drift toward movietown with lots of vague ambition, disappeared late at night. Ken and Angelo decided that they needed more time and comfort to carry out their rape and killing than their car provided, so they took her to the spare bedroom in Angelo Buono's Glendale house. The body of the girl who may or may not have worked as a prostitute was found, legs propped up and open as if ready for sex, on a sloping section of La Crescenta. Signs indicated that she had been gagged with tape and her wrists and ankles bound. The police quickly saw that two men were involved.

On November 5 it was the turn of Lissa Kastin, a serious dancer with no connection to the street world at all. Her body was found in Glendale on the hillside above a cul-de-sac.

Then, within just a few days, Los Angeles-area women everywhere knew they had something to fear. Seven women were bound, stripped, raped, sodomized, tortured, strangled, and dumped—by two terrifying figures who quickly came to be known as the "Hillside Stranglers."

Jill Barcomb, eighteen, found dead November 10.

Jane King, twenty-eight, found November 23, though she had probably been dead almost two weeks. Actress and model.

Kathleen Robinson, seventeen, found November 17.

Refinement: the men decided to try virgins next. Sonja Johnson, fourteen, found on November 20, along with her friend Dollie Cepeda, twelve. Students in a private residential Catholic school. Both wore braces on their teeth. The girls were stopped by men they thought were policemen minutes after they had lifted expensive costume jewelry from a shop. In terror at being caught, they did whatever the "policemen" asked of them—and died.

Kristina Weckler, twenty, also found November 20. An

honors art student in Pasadena. She had rejected Kenny's attentions when he lived in the same apartment building. Refinement: injection of window cleaner into her veins and placing her head in a plastic bag with a pipe leading to the gas stove.

Lauren Wagner, eighteen, found November 29. Business school student. Refinement: application of electricity to her body.

And Kenny and Angelo reveled in the publicity their deeds were receiving. They waited, catching their breath and delighting in the growing rewards offered for the capture of the ''Hillside Stranglers.'' Ken took another jaunt with the ''ride-along'' program, in a Los Angeles police car. He also made sure that Kelli always carried an alarm with her to frighten off the Hillside Stranglers if she should be approached.

Getting restless, on December 13 the two men phoned a call-girl service and asked for a prostitute to come to a vacant apartment in the same building where Ken lived. A seventeen-year-old known as Donna—real name, Kimberley Martin—who had been with the service only two days showed up at the dark apartment. Because she tried to scream and escape, they quickly gave up their plan for using the apartment and forced her to go with them to Angelo's house in Glendale. There the terrified girl lived only another brief, horrible, few minutes. This time, after the victim was found, Ken Bianchi was interviewed by the police because he was a resident of the building where the call-girl agency had sent ''Donna.''

The police saw no reason to suspect the personable young man.

More changes came quickly for Ken. He was fired for missing too much time at work after the company found out that his chemotherapy excuse was a lie. Kelli, who had moved out several weeks before, took him to her parents for Christmas but declined the chance to move back in with him. Because he had no job and could not pay his rent, he moved out of his apartment and into a house with two homosexuals, friends of Kelli's brother. To Ken's dismay, Angelo insisted that they lay off the murders for a while.

Ken filled the interim by going after high school girls who were happy to offer sex to the attractive older man with the luxurious Cadillac and an apparently endless supply of pornographic movies. Then, grotesquely, he went home to Kelli and participated in Lamaze childbirth classes with her.

But the fancy car was repossessed in February, and Ken either had to take the bus or beg for an occasional ride in the grand Excalibur that Angelo had put together out of a kit. Finally, on December 16, Cindy Lee Hudspeth, a waitress and community-college employee, walked into Angelo's shop when Ken was there, and the two decided it was killing time again, even though it was daylight. Discussing potential jobs that might interest her, the men enticed Cindy into the house. They abused her for several hours and then, after dark, killed her. They stuffed her into her own car and drove it to a canyon cliff, where they pushed it over.

Ken Bianchi's son was born a few days later. Then he was kicked out of the homosexuals' house for never having paid any of the expenses. He got a new apartment, a new job, and a new car—bought with money borrowed from Sheryl Kellison, his first girlfriend in LA. Her mother, furious at his borrowing the money, went to the police and suggested that this Kenneth Bianchi might be the Hillside Strangler. Police officers way down the line in the Strangler Task Force interviewed him briefly, found him innocuous, filed their report, and forgot him.

But the fact that the police had been to see Kenny again bothered Angelo, and he cruelly told his younger cousin that it was time to get lost. When Kenny continued to hang around, Angelo encouraged him to follow Kelli and his son to Bellingham, Washington. That encouragement finally turned into a threat to kill him if he *didn't* go!

The Bellingham Murders

Ken Bianchi left Los Angeles, where the police were putting herculean efforts into solving the murders of twelve women and girls. First, however, he advertised for psychologists, stole the credentials of one man who answered the ad, and wrote the man's college for a copy of his diploma. The man was named Steve Walker. Later, the police would assume that that was where Ken Bianchi got the name for his murderous alter ego, Steve.

Reaching Bellingham, Ken promptly took a job with a security firm, trying to demonstrate the proper responsibility for a man who was father of a young child. From the first day, he impressed his bosses with his dedication and skill, quickly becoming a specialist in electronic security systems. He stole numerous small items—the kind that people just ponder about for a moment, wondering where they might have misplaced them, and then forget. Even better, he was accepted into the Sheriff's Reserves of Whatcom County, so that he could at last really call himself a law-enforcement officer. But that's where the excitement ended for him; otherwise, the small city near the Canadian border was excruciatingly boring after Los Angeles.

Life—and death—with Angelo began to look increasingly appealing, especially after Ken admitted that he no longer found Kelli, mother of his child, the least bit interesting sexually.

Gradually, as winter in the far northern city closed in darker and more chill, he decided that it was time to enliven his life with some of the things he had enjoyed most in LA.

On Tuesday, January 9, 1979, in his security-man guise, he called Karen Mandic, a girl he knew from his first job in Bellingham the previous spring. He offered her a chance to make some good money for one brief night's work by house-sitting a house in which the security alarm was being repaired overnight. She would be paid a hundred dollars for the simple task. He blithely agreed that her roommate, Diane Wilder, was welcome to come along.

On Thursday evening, the two young women arrived at the house to which he had the key. Asking Diane to stay in the car for a moment, he led Karen inside and, finding the lights not working, took her down into the basement. Instead of looking for the fuse box, he quickly assaulted the girl, grabbed a rope he had put there earlier in the day, and strangled her. Returning outside to bring Diane in, he repeated his actions. Almost absentmindedly, he masturbated over the bodies, as if in negligent reminder that the murders were part of a sex act for him.

Missing Angelo's creative ideas, as well as the help that a second person could give in handling the bodies, Ken just carried the girls to Karen's car, stuffed them in, and drove it into a dead-end street not far away. He was feeling better than he had in some months.

What he had not anticipated was that Karen had told her boyfriend about the house-sitting appointment with Ken Bianchi. After the police found and identified the bodies, they quickly learned of Karen's date to meet Ken at the house. Then, checking Bianchi's own rented house, they found numerous stolen items. Within hours, Ken, who had long thought that his were the brains behind the fact that his and Angelo's murders had never been solved, was under arrest. The police held him on theft charges in order to give them time to check more fully into the possibility that he had murdered Karen Mandic and Diane Wilder.

In a horrible irony, the chief of police in Bellingham, an ex-priest named Terry Mangan, was a friend of the father of fourteen-year-old victim Sonja Johnson. Mangan contacted the Los Angeles police to learn more about the background of a possible murderer he had under arrest who just might have learned his skills down in LA. In California, a police officer who had served on the Hillside Strangler Task Force immediately got excited at Bianchi turning up and at the connections he was now able to make between Bianchi and the twelve victims in Los Angeles. He hurried up to Washington.

In the meantime, Ken Bianchi had the Bellingham police puzzled. When they picked him up, he gave every appearance of being eager to help them with their problem, but he also appeared genuinely to not connect himself with the murders in any way. He firmly stated that he could not remember what he had been doing the night of January 11, but was clearly disturbed at the notion that he might have been murdering two women— enough so that a psychiatric social worker was called in to keep him from committing suicide.

If the police hadn't had the clear-cut theft charges to hold Ken on, they might have taken him at face value and let him go. As it was, he was safely tucked in jail when the forensics investigators verified that some pubic hair found on Karen Mandic's body had come from Ken Bianchi. He could finally be charged with murder.

Kelli herself, in long interviews with the police, inadvertently provided many of the links they needed. She also told them about Angelo Buono, Ken's cousin and closest friend, whom she didn't like. LA detectives immediately put Angelo under surveillance. Investigators discovered among Kelli's jewelry some pieces that they knew had been owned by women who had been killed in Los Angeles.

* * *

Ken? No, Steve

Ken, Kelli, and Ken's attorney, Dean Brett, all believed that a serious mistake was being made, that Ken could not possibly be one of the Hillside Stranglers. Darcy O'Brien, author of *Two of a Kind: The Hillside Stranglers*, wrote: "Locked up safely in the Whatcom County Jail, Kenny Bianchi had little opportunity to indulge his inclinations to evil, but he could still lie. And he found several people important to his fate who were ready, for one reason or another, to believe him."

Brett started an investigation into Ken's background that soon revealed the abuse, the amnesia, the continuous wetting. On the basis of what he learned, Brett asked a famous psychiatrist known for his use of hypnosis to interrogate Kenneth Bianchi.

More than two months after his arrest, as the attorneys, the policemen from LA, and the Washington police officers watched, Ken was interviewed by Dr. John G. Watkins, who persuaded him to allow himself to be hypnotized. The two men chatted for a while, with Watkins telling Ken quite a bit about hypnosis before putting him "under," though Ken had previously read at least one book on the subject. Then, in a manner that would later cause a great deal of controversy, Dr. Watkins deliberately asked to speak to "another part of Ken that I haven't talked to, another part that maybe feels somewhat differently from the part that I've talked to."

The hypnotized suspect, speaking in a voice considerably different from his normal voice, introduced himself as

"Steve." He abruptly said, "I hate Ken!" and they quickly learned that Steve also hated anything "nice," as well as his mother.

Soon he was saying that he—Steve—was present in Ken when Ken walked into Angelo's house one night and found him killing a girl. Steve liked that and so he forced Ken to participate in the killings as a way of "getting back at his mother," although Steve proudly insisted that it was he, Steve, who did the killings, not Ken.

Steve went into great detail about the murders, providing the proofs the police needed to take to court. But the existence of a "Steve" in Kenneth Bianchi, if believed by a jury, could mean that he would be found not guilty by reason of insanity, a situation that they did not want to happen because he might eventually go free. They became certain that they could trace the generation of his multiple personality back to an idea accidentally given by the psychiatric social worker, to his own reading in psychology, to the movie *The Three Faces of Eve*, which Ken had seen years before, and finally, just two days before his first psychiatric interview, to the movie *Sybil*, which he had watched on television in his cell. Particularly from watching Sally Field play the woman who had been found to have a number of different dissociated personalities, Ken could have learned all he needed to know to carry off the pretense of being several personalities in one body.

A difficulty faced by those who were inclined to believe in the existence of the "many faces of Kenneth Bianchi" was that Dr. Watkins, in closing his interview with Ken, had planted the seeds that would let the conscious Ken begin to be aware of the existence of his evil alter ego, Steve. Watkins told him, "During the coming days and weeks, at your own speed, and in your own way, you will find out about Steve, who he is, what he has done, and what has happened. And you will find out in such a way that you can become stronger and stronger and stronger with each passing day." Thus no psychiatrist coming later saw the same Kenneth Bianchi/ Steve combination that Dr. Watkins so surprisingly met.

On March 28, a different psychiatrist conducted a long interview with Ken without using hypnosis. Ken went into a great deal more detail about his childhood, calling attention to events about which he had always had "amnesia."

Gradually, bit by bit, psychiatrist by psychiatrist—both prosecution and defense and on behalf of the court itself—a picture was built up during the following months of Kenneth Bianchi and his counterpart Steve. Steve had appeared when Kenny needed him most, to take the brunt of the punishment meted out by his mother. If she abused the rebellious Steve, Kenny himself was safe. Steve could refer to his mother as "a fuckin' cunt" and Ken would not get in trouble. After his father died, Ken's mother tried to keep him close at hand, but he cried, "I can't be Dad. I kept telling her I can't be Dad. I'm just a kid."

They also learned that there might be another personality hidden in Ken, a frightened boy named Billy who might have appeared at the time Ken's father died. Billy was aware of Steve but not of Ken and he told the police many more details about things Steve had done. Billy was also the thief within the Ken triumvirate who got a kick out of stealing things.

The interviews also revealed, as opposed to his earlier statement that he became involved in murder by walking in on Angelo killing a girl, that Steve/Ken had killed Yolanda Washington, the first victim. In addition, they discovered that when Steve killed, he was in a state of great anger that would well up inside him, anger that was relieved only by the death of a girl.

All the interviews were both taped and videotaped. The detectives who saw them, hunting for further information to use in building a case against Angelo, became convinced that Kenneth Bianchi was putting on the performance of his life, using everything he had ever learned about psychology to fool several eminent psychiatrists. Many of his statements, especially regarding actions taken during the murders, were made in the passive voice: "she was killed," "intercourse was had," "her body was taken." Several of the psychiatrists related this to what they called "objective" memory; Ken remembered things as if he were seeing them from outside rather than from having participated in them. Not all of the psychiatrists, however, were willing to admit that this was related to multiple personality, though all agreed that he was at least psychotic.

When the LA police learned that Angelo and Ken had put everything that a girl had on her—except for a couple of pieces of jewelry that Ken had taken when Angelo wasn't looking—into a plastic bag which they threw into a big trash dumpster, the investigators knew that there was little chance of ever getting much physical evidence against Angelo. They were going to have to rely in court on the testimony of self-confessed killer Steve/Ken Bianchi to put Buono out of circulation.

On October 19, 1979, a hearing on Ken Bianchi's sanity was held in the Bellingham court. Dean Brett spent long hard hours beforehand convincing Ken to plead guilty to the Washington murders and to agree to go to LA to testify against Angelo. And in return, he would not be executed; instead he would be sent to a California prison for life, saving him from the known horrors of the much tougher Washington State prison.

Brett did not know for sure, though, just what Ken would do when the time actually came to plead guilty. He might once again bring up the emphatic denials that he had expressed during his long months in the county jail.

He did plead guilty, however, and he was sentenced to two life terms in prison. Then he was immediately shipped to Los Angeles. There he pleaded guilty to five of the twelve Hillside Strangler killings and was sentenced to additional life terms. As this was going on, Angelo Buono was finally arrested on the understanding that Ken was going to testify against him.

Within days, however, Ken's own personality began to deny the things that ''Steve'' had done and that he had admitted to. He thought that perhaps he had only watched the murders and was only guilty of not preventing them.... But then perhaps they had been committed by another man entirely, with Angelo, of course.... But perhaps it was Billy, that frightened, young, additional personality, who had done the murders.

From day to day, week to week, as the prosecution prepared to try Angelo Buono, they never knew just what frame of mind their only real witness would be in. His confession revealed a lot of detail that only a murderer could have known, but if he would not corroborate it in court, most of the impact on a jury would be lost.

In a preliminary hearing in July 1981, Ken Bianchi completely denied the killings in the morning, then proudly detailed them in the afternoon. The dismayed prosecutor asked the judge to drop the case. To almost everyone's surprise, Judge Ronald M. George insisted that the case be carried on, and the California district attorney's office took charge of the prosecution.

Then began one of the longest criminal trials in United States history. On November 14, 1983, just five years after the first body was found on a Los Angeles hillside and two years after the trial started, Angelo Buono was found guilty. The jury sentenced him to life in prison without parole, perhaps because Ken Bianchi would receive nothing more or less.

On January 9, 1984, the judge confirmed the jury's sentence for Buono and sentenced Kenneth Bianchi to be sent back to Washington State to serve out his life in the harsh prison atmosphere that he had tried to avoid.

Recently, the man of many personalities has become a convert to Seventh Day Adventism and works for the chaplain at the Washington prison where he—and Steve—and Billy—will be for the rest of his life.

15

The Self-Created Golden Killer
Theodore Bundy

There was a time, way back, when I felt deep, deep guilt about even the very thought of harming someone. And yet... I had a desire to condition that out of me.

Ted Bundy

As the boy grew, he fashioned himself into a winning figure that was carefully planned, developed, and exploited to become what he wanted to be in the public eye: sophisticated, compelling, attractive—one of "the best and the brightest." But within him grew another "entity" that was just as carefully nurtured to become one of the most enigmatic and terrifying serial killers known, destroyer of at least twenty and probably many more beautiful, young lives.

* * *

First—and always—there was his mother, Louise Cowell, the oldest of three daughters of Sam Cowell of Philadelphia. She was the one who learned early to suppress the reality of her father's rages and the frequent beatings her mother sustained from him, showing only an innocent, shining face to the public. She was the one who, at seventeen years of age, showed up alone at the gates of a home for unwed mothers in Burlington, Vermont. She was the one who told a vague tale of a college-educated sailor who had had his way with her, making her pregnant and then leaving.

Theodore Robert was born on November 24, 1946. Louise left the infant at the home, unloved and unwanted during those critical weeks that psychiatrists say are vital to the development of a caring, loving, "normal" person. Louise returned to Philadelphia to argue out the merits of adoption with her father, the only member of the family allowed to have an opinion. Her father insisted that she keep the baby, and she has never admitted in public that she wanted anything else, though apparently her emotional rejection of the baby spoke for her.

She returned to her father's home, bearing the two-month-old infant whom her father professed to friends and relatives to have adopted, though few believed the story, especially when the growing Teddy, in confusion, referred to Louise as "Mommy." That sound would warm the hearts of most women, but Louise Cowell found the whole subject—and product—of her unwanted motherhood anathema, though she would have died rather than let the world know that she had never wanted her child.

Her own mother retreated into quiet depression that kept her housebound and alone.

Young Teddy learned very early to live with the dichotomy—show the world that you can be all it expects of you; deny the dark reality beneath the glowing, superficially healthy surface. No one ever explained to the child who he was or who his father was. Perhaps even as a toddler he began to suspect that his unknown father and his grandfather were one and the same person. But his grandfather was a very violent man, and so Teddy learned quickly not to ask about the possibility, just to maintain the facade that everything was for the best in this best of all possible worlds, despite whatever blacknesses he might perceive underneath the appearance. And so little Ted learned early that it was all right to lead a double life.

Myra MacPherson, writing in *Vanity Fair* after Ted Bundy was executed, related a tale told by his Aunt Julia from when Ted was about three and a half years old. Louise's younger sister, a teenager, was sound asleep one morning when she woke to find the youngster lifting her bed covers and carefully placing sharp butcher knives beside her. No one did anything about the strange act when Julia took the knives back down to the kitchen and told the family what had happened. That type of "bizarre behavior," says Dr. Dorothy Lewis, who worked with Bundy before his execution, is seen "only in very seriously traumatized children who have either themselves been the victims of extraordinary abuse or who have witnessed extreme violence among family members."

When Ted was not yet four years old, however, his great-aunt, grandfather Cowell's sister, paid for Louise and her son to move to Tacoma, Washington, where no one except one uncle knew that Teddy was illegitimate, thus making the facade easier to maintain. That might have been easier for Louise, but Teddy again got no answers as to why he had to leave the grandpa whom he loved and go, with a mother who clearly didn't want him, to a strange place, or why, when he knew his last name was Cowell, it suddenly became Nelson (a name she made up), and then just as suddenly—when Louise married an army cook—it became Bundy.

Ted never had any real liking for his stepfather, Johnnie Culpepper Bundy, and instead turned his admiration on his great-uncle, Jack Cowell, a well-to-do professor who lived a cultured life in surroundings that appeared luxurious to the growing boy. Very early Ted came to resent the fact that his stepfather's pay would not bring him all the things he wanted. So even as a young child, Ted set his sights on becoming a man like his uncle, while envying Jack's son for getting to live as he did. He particularly hated the uninteresting, inexpensive cars that Johnnie drove. Ted's quest for something more than his immediate family had became even more important when Johnnie forced him to spend much of his spare time harvesting vegetables in the big fields of central Washington, a task which he hated and resented, regardless of the fact that it brought additional money into the household.

The Bundys produced two stepsisters and two stepbrothers for Ted, the last one not coming until he was in his midteens. Apparently he did not resent having to babysit for the young ones, and he enjoyed the adulation they gave their fascinating older brother.

Youthful Discovery

Several important things happened as Ted entered adolescence. First and foremost, it was probably at that time that he learned he was illegitimate. Through the years he told several different stories about when and how he learned that all-important fact. If he learned it at that age, it was either through finding his birth certificate, which, at that time, blatantly recorded illegitimacy, or through a nasty cousin angrily calling him "a bastard" and meaning it literally. From that time on, he both became a loner and set himself on a path of achievement so that he could stand out and pretend to be something that he knew at heart he wasn't. Although he already knew that his mother didn't love him, at that time he probably rejected her, too. That rejection, however, would have been subconscious; more consciously, he openly rebelled against his stepfather. Somehow, the knowledge that he was illegitimate turned an open, enthusiastic child into an introverted, withdrawn, overly sensitive, resentful teenager who stopped growing emotionally.

Secondly, he discovered sex and the self-absorption of masturbation. Friends from junior high school later said that Ted Bundy was known for hiding away in closets and bathrooms at school to masturbate. Everyone knew he did it. Along with that, he discovered pornography, the more violent the better.

Just before he was executed, Bundy called Dr. James Dobson, the Christian family therapist known for his TV and radio series called *Focus on the Family*, and asked him to come see him. Bundy had a message that he wanted to get to the American people: that pornography can "reach out and snatch a kid out of any house today." He said that in prison he had met numerous rapists and killers and that "without exception every one of them was . . . consumed by an addiction to pornography."

At the time, he was busily trying to explain to anyone who would listen all the factors that went into making him a killer, hoping that someone would manage to get the courts or the governor to grant a stay of execution. Because of that, his plea against pornography was disregarded by the media. However, it is likely that a young kid becoming fascinated with sex and studying the hardest of hard-core pornography might well come to accept that violence is a natural concomitant of sex.

Dr. Dorothy Lewis thinks that the absorption in pornography overlaid a more fundamental absorption. After speaking with Bundy that same week as Dr. Dobson, she told Myra MacPherson that she learned "how *very, very early* he had a fascination with stories of murders and murderers and death. At that early time, the fascination was not with pornography. Later on it fused."

It is probable that as Bundy entered his teens, a time when a child might be gone from the house for lengthy periods without someone looking for him, he began to prowl at night, looking through other people's windows, hoping to see women undressing. This voyeurism remained an activity of his all his life, and during his killing years it served as his means of finding sleeping women to attack.

In addition to discovering his illegitimacy and sex, Ted most likely learned to be adept at thievery. If his stepfather couldn't give him something, he found ways to take it. He became an adept skier, and was particularly enchanted with the ski life. He had the best equipment (stolen) and a constant supply of lift tickets (forged). Stealing remained one of Bundy's primary ways of dealing with life as long as he was out of prison. Even when he had nothing, as in the weeks he lived in Florida after escaping from prison in Colorado, he lived high on the hog by stealing everything he needed, either directly or by using stolen credit cards.

In his teen years, Ted, who would later have women swooning over him, held himself fairly isolated from other young people, although he was an officer in his church youth group. Knowing that he didn't stand out much socially, he made it a point to stand out in class. He didn't date much, and, when he did, it was usually the girls, already feeling some of his superficial charisma, who did the asking.

The University Years

Bundy started college in 1966 at the University of Puget Sound, in Tacoma, where he could live at home. His special pleasure was the ten-year-old Volkswagen he bought, the first of two he would own. Although he was invited to join a fraternity, his social, upper-middle-class persona—the one he would soon be carefully constructing—was not yet polished enough to overcome his insecurity in the face of the boisterous and confident fraternity brothers he encountered, and he declined the invitation. Becoming interested in Asian Studies—a field small enough to allow him to really stand out—he transferred the following year to the University of Washington, in Seattle. Moving into a coed dorm, he began to attract girls with his apparent self-confidence, wit, intelligence, and even suavity, but he paid little attention to them until he met the girl who was to play a major role in what Ted Bundy became.

Ann Rule, in *The Stranger Beside Me*, called her Stephanie. Stephen G. Michaud and Hugh Aynesworth, in *The Only Living Witness*, called her Marjorie. Richard W. Larsen, in *Bundy: The Deliberate Stranger*, called her Cas. And Michael Daly, writing in *Rolling Stone*, gave her a name that indicated her class: Ruth Arista. Daughter of a well-to-do Mormon businessman, The Girl, as we'll call her, was cultured, traveled, exquisitely dressed, and, in toto, all the things that Ted Bundy yearned in his heart to be. Shoring up his sleek outer image, Ted went after the tall, slender girl with the long, shiny, brown hair, which she wore parted in the middle so that it hung sleekly down past her shoulders.

And he got her... at least, he got her for the better part of a year. With her encouragement, Ted, who had become interested in politics when participating in a mock election in high school, became active as a volunteer in the state campaign to gain Nelson Rockefeller the

Republican nomination. They skied a lot, and played. Ted even took The Girl to his home in Tacoma, his desire to show her off to his family overcoming the desire to keep the reality of his lower-middle-class home hidden. She kept telling him that none of that mattered.

In the summer of 1968, however, The Girl let him know that she was through. The traits that had at first seemed fun to her had become annoying, his lack of any clear-cut goals disturbing in a long-term relationship, especially for a girl who expected to keep on living the good life to which she had been raised.

The loss of The Girl shattered Ted Bundy. He lost his ambition, his desire to stand out in class, even his carefully constructed image, and dropped out of school. After working for a while as driver and bodyguard to a candidate for lieutenant governor who lost his bid for election, Ted finally took off in early 1969 on an odyssey across the country. He visited relatives, took courses— never completed—at Temple University, and ventured to Burlington, Vermont, where, confirming what he had known, he looked up his birth certificate, marked, in no uncertain terms, "illegitimate." It's likely that he again wondered if his grandfather could be his father.

As if he needed to also reconfirm other things, Ted went to San Francisco, where The Girl was working. He saw her briefly, but only long enough for her to say again that they had no future together.

Constructing the Double Ted

Ted Bundy returned to Seattle with a new determination. If he couldn't be something special through his birth, he would become something so special that The Girl would have to take notice.

He took a room in a private home, where he would remain for the next five years, and furnished it to his satisfaction with stolen goods. Returning to college, he changed his major to psychology and quickly made a name for himself as an honors student. He also quickly acquired a new girlfriend, Elizabeth "Kendall," who remained devoted to him until long after he was a prisoner. The divorced medical secretary with a small daughter would eventually tell the story of their relationship in *The Phantom Prince: My Life with Ted Bundy*, under the pseudonym of Kendall.

More than ever, Ted was leading a double life. On the surface he was becoming a sophisticated, learned, social being, who attracted attention whenever he wanted to. On the darker side, he became even more involved in theft and voyeurism. He became adept at changing his appearance with just a quick recomb of the hair, a different shirt, a new way of walking or speaking, even the addition of a false mustache, which he took to wearing frequently. Liz, with whom he spent much of his time, learned never to question his strange hours, his lies, or the reason that he kept a crowbar handy.

In the fall of 1971, Ted took a forty-hour crisis-prevention course and went to work for the Seattle Crisis Clinic, serving as a paid nighttime crisis counselor. He was frequently on duty with crime writer Ann Rule, who was a volunteer counselor. He would move in and out of her life for the next eighteen years, until he was executed for murder. She would later write that in the crisis job Ted was patient and caring with the people who called. Other people reported that he was often abrupt, tending to order the lonely and even suicidal callers to straighten themselves up.

Bundy graduated the following spring. His psychology professors were more than happy to write glowing recommendations for him to attend law school, but his law aptitude test scores were too low and he was turned down. He took a job as an outpatient counselor at a hospital. According to a female counselor he worked and played with, the two of them spent a great deal of time taking long drives through the Cascade Mountains, where some of his victims would later be found. He told her that he was trying to find an elderly relative's home. Liz Kendall never knew that he was spending long hours with other women.

Not truly liking his job, Ted volunteered once again to work for a political candidate, Republican governor Dan Evans. He charmed the press, kowtowed to those over him in the political structure, delighted in serving as a spare male at elegant dinners, and, all in all, succeeded in strengthening his facade as the Golden Boy. He took the opportunity to replace his old VW with a newer one, a bronze-colored '68 model whose front passenger seat could be easily removed.

Following the November 1972 election, when his candidate regained the statehouse, Ted applied for law school again, this time with a recommendation written by the governor himself. He was accepted at the University of Utah for the following autumn. While waiting for that to start, he worked with a major government study concerning crime recording, and with the Republican state committee.

While he studied criminal statistics during the day, he was working at night to contribute to them. Step by step, the "entity," as Bundy called his darker, sex-and-violence-absorbed self, began to consume the Golden Boy.

At first, he just peered in through windows at women. Then, one night after drinking fairly heavily, he followed a woman as she walked home from a bar. He began to fantasize, not about raping her, but about attacking her with a club. He grabbed a piece of two-by-four, dashed ahead of her, and lay in wait. He was just about to hit her when she turned into the doorway of her home.

Afterward, he was horrified at what he had almost done, at what he now knew he was capable of doing. But he was exhilarated by it, too. He later told Michaud and Aynesworth (in the third person in which he confessed): ". . . The frenzied desire that seized him, un, really seemed to usher in a new dimension to the, that part of himself that was obsessed with, or otherwise enamored with, violence and women and sexual activity—a composite kind of thing."

Gradually the fear wore off, and Ted tried it again, this time actually attacking a woman as she unlocked her car. She fell to the ground screaming, and he had to run.

Again the reaction wore off, more quickly this time.

But now Bundy let his intellectual side revamp his plans. He knew that if he kept his activities to the street, he would undoubtedly be caught. If he were to go inside a house, where it wouldn't matter if a woman screamed, he would be much safer. He followed another woman home, watched her as she prepared for bed, found an open door, and sneaked into her bedroom. However, she woke and did indeed scream, and Ted ran.

The major breakthrough had been made, however. He knew he could enter houses for sex and violence, just as he had earlier learned that he could enter for theft. He knew, too, that the urge would come on him again. When Michaud and Aynesworth asked him to describe that urge, Bundy, intellectualizing, said that the "spark . . . that ignited the subliminal juices was not one born of anger or hostility toward women or anything of that particular nature," but, instead, "it was a high degree of anticipation, of excitement, of arousal. It was like an *adventuristic* kind of thing."

In the meantime, before starting law school in 1973, Ted Bundy had a point to prove. He flew to San Francisco to see The Girl, who had rejected him as insecure and immature. This time she discovered that Ted Bundy was indeed the Golden Boy. She found in him all the things she wanted in a man. He was moving with the right people and was apparently in control of his life. When he left to return to school, she was already anticipating that they would spend their lives together.

At the last-minute urging of a friend, Ted switched to the law school at the University of Puget Sound in

Tacoma, while continuing to live in Seattle. However, he found the whole place dull, the other students beneath his dignity, and the law school, which decidedly lacked the Ivy League look, not worthy of the new Ted Bundy. He soon began to fail in his classes, though neither Liz nor his family knew it, and he kept up the facade through the winter months. Without telling anyone, he reapplied to the University of Utah (which he had turned down, citing as the reason a nonexistent automobile accident) and was accepted for the following fall.

The Girl eagerly came to Seattle to see Ted over the Christmas vacation of 1973, while Liz was away in Utah with her own family. He borrowed a friend's apartment for the visit. The disintegrating Ted, however, had to dredge up memories of what he had been like the previous summer and put on an act. He was able to pretend still to be the Golden Boy, but the effort was exhausting.

The Girl flew elsewhere for the actual Christmas holiday, thinking herself engaged, and then returned to Ted's side for the New Year. Each day that passed, she expected him to say, "Let's set the date," but instead he backed off. Finally, as she was leaving, he said flatly that he didn't think the two of them would work. Stunned and bewildered, the woman who had previously rejected him flew back to San Francisco, herself rejected.

Perhaps his mind had already been on his next "adventure." Two days later, in the early hours of January 4, 1974, Ted ventured into the basement bedroom of an eighteen-year-old student he had followed and attacked her with a metal rod that he forced from the frame of her bed. He didn't rape her; instead, he thrust the rod up her vagina in one grotesque final gesture. She was found some hours later, unconscious, and she remained in a coma for several weeks, awaking to amnesia of the episode and permanent brain damage.

It would be only a small step further to make Ted Bundy a murderer.

The Murdering "Entity"

On the night of January 31, Bundy was wandering around with his "entity" in control. Passing a house where he had frequently seen several attractive students going in and out, he tried an outer basement door and found it unlocked. The house was quiet, so he wandered in and prowled around. Looking into one room, he saw the tall, slender figure of Lynda Ann Healy, the twenty-one-year-old, sexy-sounding ski reporter on Seattle radio. Striking her as she slept, he knocked her unconscious.

In the still of the wee hours, he neatly made up her bed to conceal the blood she had shed, gathered her clothes, and moved the unconscious girl out to his car, out of which the passenger seat could so conveniently be removed. Bound and gagged, she lay beside him as he drove out of town. In the vague, third-person confession that Bundy made to Michaud and Aynesworth, he said, "The sexual gratification probably preceded the point where the final decision was made to kill the individual. . . . Assuming . . . that he drove directly up into the wilds, and assuming a fairly continuous progression of events, it probably would have [taken] a little more than a few hours.'' He also noted: ''A nominally normal individual who has become somewhat subordinate to bizarre desires and abducts a woman and kills her, finds himself in a great deal of panic.''

(Despite these statements about Lynda Healy's murder, Bundy himself said at another time that his first murder actually took place at least eight months earlier, in May 1973, though no specific death at that time has been tied to him.)

Bundy remained in a state of anxiety for several weeks, afraid that Lynda Healy's body would be found because he had not had the courage to bury it. However, her whereabouts would remain a complete mystery for thirteen months, until her body showed up with several others in the Cascade mountains east of Seattle.

Gradually the tension he felt, as well as the certainty that he would never kill again, subsided, and Bundy's ''entity'' began to ''regenerate itself.'' His intellect was able to contribute more to this effort, however, by making him go outside of Seattle for the next events. He knew that his victims would not get much publicity if they were not linked together. Because of his decisions to spread the murders around and to hide the victims long distances from where they lived, Bundy was setting out on a pattern that would clock many miles on his trusty little VW. However, being less intelligent on this matter, he used credit cards so often that he would later be seen to have left a paper trail behind him.

On March 12, on the campus of The Evergreen State

College, at Olympia, nineteen-year-old music student Donna Manson set out in the evening to walk to a jazz concert. She never arrived and she was never seen again.

Up to this time, student Ted Bundy, though he was disappointed in the UPS law school, had meticulously attended all his classes. But now he was missing classes and failing tests. In mid-April he dropped out of school completely. All his energy was focused on murder. He did not even have anything to offer Liz Kendall sexually. Not even tying her up with nylon panty hose—one of his favorite activities—could arouse him.

Another five weeks passed. Then Bundy went to Ellensburg, one hundred and twenty miles from Seattle, the home of Central Washington State College. He hunted around for a few hours, introducing himself to another refinement that his intellect had suggested to him. With one arm in a sling, he had to ask for the help of a pretty girl or two to get his books into his VW. One girl agreed to help, but something "strange" about the tall, good-looking guy caused her to drop his books on the hood of the car and run.

Disgruntled, Bundy hung around until evening, when he saw a voluptuous, long-haired blond walking into the twenty feet of darkness under a railway trestle. The body of Susan Rancourt, a freshman biology major who almost never went out alone at night, would be found thirteen months later lying near that of Lynda Healy.

Also found nearby at that time were the remains of Kathy Parks, a student at Oregon State University in Corvallis (amazingly, a full two hundred and fifty miles from Seattle), who had disappeared May 6, and Brenda Ball, a community college student in Burien, who had last been seen June 1. She had spent the evening at a tavern until closing time, when a man with his arm in a sling had been seen in the parking lot. Bundy later admitted that he had chatted with her and offered to go to another tavern with her. He used the excuse of needing to pick up some class work as a way of driving out of town to where he could "accost her without any fear of attracting attention."

This time Bundy, using the full blast of the Golden Boy charisma, took Brenda Ball home to his own apartment. There he fed her plenty of liquor and raped her. Bundy told his own story: "After the first sexual encounter, gradually his sexual desire builds back up and joins, as it were, these other unfulfilled desires—this other need to totally possess her, after she's passed out, as she lay there in a state somewhere between coma and sleep, he strangled her to death." He apparently kept her body there for some days, occasionally having to hide it in the closet, before taking it to the mountains. Apparently he even washed her hair and applied fresh makeup.

Still planning to go to the University of Utah in the fall, Ted abandoned Liz and found a summer job in Olympia, working with the state's Department of Emergency Services. The DES was assisting in the investigation of the female students so strangely missing from several Washington colleges, though his task was to prepare the next year's budget. Even with so much of his life now bound up in being a rapist and murderer, Bundy the Golden Boy caught the attention of his fellow workers. They all found him charming, none more so than Carole Ann Boone. Eventually, when he was in prison in Florida, she would become his wife and bear his daughter.

In Olympia, something made Ted Bundy change his way of working—not that he stopped killing and not that he stopped being attracted to the long-haired girls, but, as far as the authorities could tell later, he stopped using his "killing ground" in the mountains. He also returned to his original hunting grounds, Seattle.

On June 11, just after midnight, eighteen-year-old Georgeann Hawkins disappeared during the seconds it would take her to walk the forty feet from behind a fraternity house where she had been chatting with a boy leaning out a window, to the door of her sorority house on the campus of the University of Washington. Another student reported seeing a young man with his leg in a full cast who, because of his crutches, was having a difficult time carrying a briefcase. No trace of Georgeann was ever seen again.

On July 3, police from all over western Washington gathered to share what information they had on the murders and disappearances of attractive, long-haired, single students. The press made a big play of the meeting, a fact that urged Bundy to act again—and even more dramatically.

On the weekend of July 14, Ted, ostensibly home from work sick with a cold, went to Lake Sammamish State Park, a popular swimming place. Late in the unusually clear and bright morning, his arm in a sling, he walked up to a girl about to join the 40,000 others in the park and asked for her help in getting his boat onto his car. There was no boat, and the girl, puzzled, left, but later saw him with another girl, one whose picture would soon be in the newspaper.

Janice Ann Ott, a probation caseworker whose husband was away on a special training course, responded to Bundy's polite request for help. People lying in the grass nearby heard him introduce himself as "Ted," and for the first time an identity, slight though it was, was attached to the killer. Janice's absence was not noted until the next day, when she failed to show up for work.

Four hours later, as some of the heat of the summer day was dissipating, Ted Bundy returned to the park. This time he stopped nineteen-year-old Denise Naslund, who was returning from the public restroom to where her boyfriend lay in the sun. An hour later Bundy was talking on the telephone to Liz Kendall. The police hunt for Denise began at dusk.

At last the police had a possibly genuine name and an oldish brownish Volkswagen, plus artist's sketches developed by girls who had chosen not to go with "Ted" to help him with his boat. Some people at Bundy's office joked with him that the sketch of "Ted" published in the newspaper looked like him, and even Liz started to feel a question niggling at the back of her mind. Several people, including both Ann Rule and Liz Kendall, quietly entered Ted Bundy's name in the police list of people who resembled the sketch, but there were ultimately thousands of men's names on that list and far too few officers to investigate them all.

The bodies of the two girls were found in September in the woods about two miles from the park. But, most horribly, a *spare* human leg bone was also found. Who it came from, or where the rest of the body was, has never been solved—consequently, we can never know just how many attractive girls, who wore their long hair parted in the middle, Ted Bundy murdered.

Before those bodies were found, Ted closed out that phase of his life by crossing Puget Sound to Vancouver, where he kidnapped Carol Valenzuela. Her body, along with that of another girl who remained unidentified, was found in October south of Olympia.

The Killer Goes Elsewhere

Ted drove to Salt Lake City and registered at the university law school. He quickly became a campus security officer, as well as the lover of several girls on campus.

The murders began again, this time with a twist. Within little more than a month, four high school girls disappeared. The only two who were found had been beaten on the head, raped, sodomized, and strangled.

Then came the first victim who got away without suffering any physical damage. On November 8, eighteen-year-old Carol DaRonch was at a shopping mall in Murray, a suburb of Salt Lake City, when Ted Bundy, who had been following her since she got out of her car, came up to her and said that someone had reported seeing a man trying to break into her car. Assuming that he was an official of some sort, she followed him out into the parking lot, where she quickly checked her car and saw that nothing was missing. Leading her to another part of the parking lot, he ignored her increasingly disturbed questions, though he did introduce himself as "Officer Roseland." Doubting the wisdom of the move, she got into a rather battered Volkswagen to go to police head-quarters, only to find herself being driven in the wrong direction. She tried frantically to get out of the car, but he fought her and managed to get a handcuff on one wrist. In the process, he was scratched enough to bleed slightly. He held a gun on her briefly but had to throw it down to pick up his crowbar, at which point she managed to kick him in the groin and run away. A couple in a passing car saw the terrified girl and took her to the police station.

As Carol DaRonch was telling her story, Ted Bundy was already at a high school where a play was being produced that evening. In the audience was seventeen-year-old Debra Kent with her parents. She left at inter-mission to go and pick up her brother, but she was never seen again. A handcuff key was found in the school parking lot.

The law student with the glowing recommendation from the governor of Washington state was not living up to his press notices. Once again, Bundy was having a difficult time concentrating on, or even caring about, graduate school. Treasuring the January vacation, he went to Colorado to ski.

On the night of January 12, 1976, Caryn Campbell, who was at the Wildwood Inn near Aspen with her fiancé and his two children, disappeared within minutes of walking toward her second-floor room within sight of some men standing by the elevator. Her body was not found until five weeks later.

Leaving Colorado, Bundy joined Liz Kendall in Seattle for a week's vacation, then returned to school.

On March 1, two forestry students found a human skull on Taylor Mountain in the Cascades. Investigators soon found the remains of at least four girls who had disappeared more than a year before in Washington and Oregon. Two weeks later, while the press was still speculating wildly about the mountain being the site of occult ritual killings, Ted returned to Colorado, this time to Vail. On the fifteenth, Julie Cunningham, a clerk and ski instructor, disappeared on a brief walk to meet some friends in a bar. On April 6 a girl disappeared at Grand Junction, Colorado. On July 1 another girl disappeared from Farmington, Utah.

Ted, who was drinking more and more, managed to finish his classes in Salt Lake City, though his grades were barely adequate. During a week he spent with Liz in June, the long-involved pair decided to get married in six months. But everything would have changed greatly by then.

On August 16, a very high Ted Bundy was driving through Granger, a suburb of Salt Lake. The erratic way he was driving caught the attention of an off-duty police-man. Ted would probably have just been questioned and warned, but he chose to try to flee from the police car, running two stop signs while trying to get rid of some marijuana he had in the car. The policeman caught him and soon found himself curious about the fact that the front passenger seat was missing. Asking for permission to search the car (which Bundy later maintained the officer never actually requested), the policeman soon found a crowbar, an ice pick, a ski mask, rope and wire, and—most strangely—a mask made out of panty hose. Certain that he had found a burglar's tools, he arrested Ted Bundy for evading an officer, expecting that the charge would be changed later, though he had no suspicion how incredible those charges would later become.

In Official Hands

The "Golden Boy" coming to the fore, glib Ted Bundy appeared to have an answer for all the police officers' questions, and he was released on his own recognizance. Six days later, however, the charge of possession of burglary tools was added, not so much because the police were afraid he might have been stealing, but because they suspected that they had found the man who had tried to kidnap Carol DaRonch. Even though he no longer had a mustache, she was able to pick him out of the photographs she was shown.

The name Theodore Bundy was familiar to at least one police detective. Jerry Thompson had received a list from Seattle detective Bob Keppel months earlier when the Utah disappearances were seen to resemble those of Washington State. On that list was Ted Bundy's name, along with a note of his connections to the governor. Bundy was put under continuous surveillance, his apartment was searched (though nothing of great significance was found), and even his credit-card spending history was investigated. The latter would eventually show that he had been in the vicinity of all the murders, even when he claimed that he hadn't. Even the press began to pick up on the fact that the police were investigating a possible slayer of many beautiful young women, the one usually referred to as "Seattle Ted."

Bundy took the opportunity of being out of jail to sell his Volkswagen to a teenager. He also, just before appearing in a police lineup, got his hair cut short. He approached the lineup with confidence, certain that nothing wrong could be happening to the Golden Boy. But on October 2, he was picked out of the lineup by DaRonch and two women who had seen Bundy at the high school from which Debra Kent had disappeared. He was arrested for attempted kidnapping and attempted murder. There would be no more Bundy murders for two and a half years.

Fearful of being attacked by his fellow inmates, Bundy tried to stay invisible while he was in jail—at least to other prisoners; he was reveling in the publicity he was getting beyond the walls of the jail. After seven weeks, his bail was reduced to an amount that his still-incredulous family could handle. His friends, too, were completely disbelieving. Many of them gathered to build the "Ted Bundy Defense Fund." When he appeared in court again in late November 1975, his "dominant personality" (the name he gave the "Golden Boy") was in full control, and he even joked with the press. He later told Michaud and Aynesworth: "I was trying to project an image. I was feeling proud of myself. That's when I started to be pleased about fucking with the press. From then on, it was a lot of fun."

The investigations into the man now out on bail went deeper, into every activity and date making up Ted Bundy's lives—both the "dominant personality" and the "entity." No one he had ever known was exempt from conversations with detectives. Gradually they put together a list of at least thirty-five points that were relevant to the murders of seventeen girls over the past two years. They varied from as concrete as the fact that his blood type matched the blood found on Carol DaRonch's jacket to as general as the information that he had frequently gone hiking in the area of the Cascades where the "killing ground" had been found.

His trial on the kidnapping charge began on February 23, 1976, in Salt Lake City. Bundy had elected to be tried by a single judge, rather than a jury, confident that he could charm any one man into finding him innocent. But four days later that judge found him guilty. Instead of sentencing him, the judge called for a thorough, ninety-day psychological diagnostic evaluation of Bundy.

In June a psychiatric hearing was held, at which the psychiatrists had to agree that Ted Bundy was fundamentally "normal," that insanity played no role in the kidnapping attempt. He was sentenced to one to fifteen years in the Utah state prison. It was anticipated that he would probably be paroled in eighteen months.

Ted became a prison lawyer, making friends with the other inmates because he could help them with their legal problems. His moods while in jail ranged, as they had for many years, from the manic, during which he worked on proving that everyone was wrong but him, to the completely depressed, when he appeared to be convinced that suicide was his only answer.

The detectives continued their work, and by the end of October had put together enough evidence to charge Bundy with the murder of Caryn Campbell at the Wildwood Inn. On January 28, 1977, he was moved to the county jail at Aspen, Colorado. He was there almost a year, gradually taking complete charge of his own defense, convinced that everyone he dealt with was inept. Because he served as his own lawyer, he was granted unlimited telephone privileges, access to the law library, expenses, and office equipment, all of which added up to keeping him Ted Bundy, Golden Boy at work, once again.

At least that was the facade he was presenting. In reality, he was busy planning his escape. On June 7, he was driven to the courthouse for a hearing on whether the death penalty should be presented as an alternative in the upcoming trial. During the break, using his lawyer persona, Ted went to the law library—and escaped through the window. But the weather, the FBI, the police, and the public were all against him, and six days later he was recaptured, with escape, felony, and car-theft charges added.

Moved to a different jail, Bundy continued both his law work and his plans for escape. He spent long nighttime hours cutting an escape hole above the foot-square mounting plate for a light in the ceiling. He deliberately lost considerable weight so that he would have no trouble getting through the small hole. In late December, he found that he could get into the ceiling, through a crawl space, and then down into a jailer's private apartment. On New Year's Eve, when the jailer and his wife went to a movie, Ted Bundy made his second escape.

He drove a stolen car to a mountain pass, hitchhiked into Vail, took a bus to Denver, flew to Chicago, took a train to Ann Arbor, Michigan, which turned out not to be the college town he was looking for, and on January 8 arrived at the bus station in Tallahassee, Florida. There it began all over again.

Death of a Golden Boy

Ted Bundy became Chris M. Hagen and moved into a rather grubby room on the edge of the Florida State University campus. As each day passed, he swore that he was going to go job hunting, but instead he yielded to the "entity" and slept during the day while prowling the streets at night. He stole numerous items, including credit cards, which provided all his meals so that he wouldn't have to use his small cache of money. He dined well, even luxuriously, using a different credit card in each restaurant and usually only in the immediate hours after stealing it so that it hadn't been reported stolen yet.

It was only six days before Bundy's need to rape and kill, held in abeyance for more than two years, overtook him again. In preparation, he stole a white Dodge van, and on Saturday, January 14, 1978, Bundy went to a disco called Sherrod's, which happened to be next door to the Chi Omega sorority house. He was seen there, watching the girls who came in and out. Sometime around three in the morning, he entered the Chi O house and began to creep around, savoring the feeling of superiority that he had not enjoyed for so long.

One student arriving home about that time got a brief glimpse of his profile as he crouched by the front door. As he left the house, she saw that he had a three-foot-long club in his hand. She woke a friend, and they stood in the hallway discussing whether they should react to what might just have been a boyfriend making a late exit. But just then Karen Chandler stumbled out of her room, bleeding profusely from a heavily battered face. As one girl called the police, the others found Karen's roommate, also seriously wounded. Neither knew what had happened; they had been attacked as they slept.

It wasn't until after the police arrived that Lisa Levy and Margaret Bowman were found. Lisa had been raped and sodomized with an aerosol bottle. Her right nipple had been bitten almost through, and a double human bite was found deeply puncturing her buttock. It was that bite mark that would eventually send the otherwise very careful Theodore Bundy to the electric chair.

Ted had left the Chi O house and walked down the street, still carrying the club of wood he had used. A man saw him before Bundy's "entity," still not sated, entered a small duplex about three blocks away. There he attacked Cheryl Thomas, a dance student. Her neighbors on the other side of the house, awakened by strange noises, called the police. They found her almost unconscious, bludgeoned about the head, but not attacked sexually. The girl who wanted to dance would suffer a permanent loss of equilibrium and deafness from the blows to her head.

During the next two weeks, Bundy went on a spending spree throughout the region, charging hundreds of dollars' worth of items—including, strangely, thirty pairs of socks—to various stolen credit cards. But the thievery and shopping were no substitute for what his entity wanted, to kill, an urge fed by drugs and alcohol.

In the second week of February, Bundy began traveling again. On the ninth, in Lake City, near Jacksonville, he was hanging around a junior high school when he saw twelve-year-old Kim Leach leave her outdoor physical education class. She had to return to her previous classroom to get her forgotten purse. She did that and was returning to gym class when Bundy intercepted her. She was not found until two months later, when her body appeared in a state park more than thirty miles away.

Ted returned to Tallahassee, where his landlord was demanding rent, and prepared to leave Florida. But this Ted Bundy was not the one of previous years, who had been meticulous in his planning and in his destruction of any clues that might lead the police to him. At 1:00 A.M., many hours after Bundy had planned to leave, a curious policeman stopped him as he was locking a Toyota that he had stolen. There on the floor was the license plate off the stolen white van, which he had neglected to dispose of. As the officer was running a check on the number, Ted ran away. There was no pursuit that night, and he slept in his own bed, still planning to leave the next day. But the "entity" was now in control, and the "entity" was unable to get up the energy to flee. On Sunday, February 12, Bundy stole another car, his own personal favorite—a Volkswagen. He finally packed up his belongings and left Tallahassee.

He spent the following four days driving and drinking, coming within a hairsbreadth of being arrested several times, but each time his Golden Boy image gave him a chance to flee. Finally, on Valentine's Day, he was stopped by an alert deputy who checked the license plate and learned the car had been stolen. Bundy fought him, but he was no longer the physically fit young man he had been in the past.

"I wish you had killed me," he mumbled, and, as they neared the jail, Bundy asked the deputy, "If I run from you at the jail, then will you kill me?"

It took the state of Florida eleven years to fulfill Ted Bundy's request. During most of that time, Bundy the Golden Boy–lawyer managed to keep the state hopping, by introducing every way that he could think of to delay first his trials, then his appeals, finally the date set for his execution.

But on January 24, 1989, Theodore Robert Bundy, destroyer of lives, died in the electric chair.

His primary legacy was the National Center for the Analysis of Violent Crime, created for just such situations as Bundy presented—deaths, kidnappings, and rapes in a variety of states, which, in prior years, would probably not have joined efforts in the pursuit of a common killer. Also because of him, police files are no longer purged of missing-persons reports after a certain period of time, because of the dreadful possibility that those missing may turn up years later as the victims of a serial murderer.

In the days before he was put to death, Bundy confessed to thirty killings, some of which closed the files on old cases. In 1990, the FBI was still pursuing total knowledge of Ted Bundy's movements over a ten-year-period in the hope of solving other murders.

Stephen Michaud and Hugh Aynesworth, who spent many long hours with the killer during the years he was on Death Row and who came closer than anyone to learning the details of the creature that Bundy had created, wrote: "The idea of Ted Bundy preys on the mind. He [was] his own abstraction, a lethal absurdity masquerading as a man."

**THERE ARE CRIMES OF PASSION...
CRIMES OF THE HEART...**

**AND THEN THERE ARE THOSE
CRIMES TOO UNSPEAKABLE
TO UNDERSTAND.**

ABANDONED
PRAYERS
Gregg Olsen

The shocking true story of obsession,
murder, and "Little Boy Blue."

A Popular Library Paperback
coming in December 1990